# Good Cooking

# Marguerite Patten

# Good Cooking:

## The Second Piccolo Cookbook

Illustrated by Eileen Strange
and Anni Axworthy

**A Piccolo Original**
Piccolo Books

First published 1973 by Pan Books Ltd as
*The Second Piccolo Cook Book*
This revised and extended version first published 1985
by Pan Books Ltd,
Cavaye Place, London SW10 9PG

9 8 7 6 5 4 3 2 1

© Marguerite Patten 1973, 1985

Illustrations © Eileen Strange 1973
Additional illustrations ©
Anni Axworthy 1985

ISBN 0 330 28721 4

Printed and bound in Great Britain by
Richard Clay (The Chaucer Press) Ltd, Bungay, Suffolk

# Contents

# Introduction

Here is a cookery book to follow **The Piccolo Cookbook.**
The recipes are quite different, but they are still planned so
you can cook them yourselves, without any trouble. They
are easy, not too expensive, and very good to eat.

This book will help you to cook:

Supper dishes and snacks; some of them can be prepared in
just a few minutes, special vegetable and vegetarian dishes
together with ideas for packed meals and some dishes from
other countries. A complete dinner with hints to make it
easy to do. Interesting puddings and desserts, including
home-made ice cream and lots of ideas using ice cream.
Cakes and buns and biscuits of all kinds.

Please read the first few pages before you begin cooking;
they remind you of the special words and tools used in
cookery and they also tell you about the work food does in
keeping us strong and healthy. On pages 14, 15 and 16 is
information that tells you about using modern equipment
such as a food processor, liquidizer (blender) and a
microwave cooker. These are mentioned in various recipes
too.

I hope you like these recipes. Follow the instructions
carefully; if anything is in italics in a recipe, it means that it
is especially important. I have not reminded you about
warming plates and dishes in every recipe, but this is
important too. *Use oven gloves or an oven cloth to hold hot
dishes*.

Good luck and good cooking!

**Marguerite Patten**

# Some tools you will use

Your hands are important 'tools' in cooking, so wash them well before you handle food.

Here are some of the other tools (often called utensils) mentioned in the recipes:

**Basins and bowls:** you will need a nice big mixing bowl (never try to mix ingredients in too small a bowl, it is very difficult!) and some smaller basins for whisking egg, whipping cream and so on.

**Cake tins:** there are many sorts of cake tins, but for the recipes in this book you will need a baking tray, patty tins, paper cake cases and a sandwich tin.

**A colander:** is used for straining vegetables.

**Frying pans and saucepans:** make sure you choose them large enough for the amount of food. If you have non-stick pans, ask a grown-up how to take care of them, for they are spoiled by careless use and incorrect cleaning. A special kind of frying pan or saucepan is known as a wok; this is chiefly used for Chinese dishes but is extremely good for other cooking too, see pages 112–15.

**A grater:** is used for making pieces of cheese, lemon rind, etc., smaller. The picture shows the most usual kind. If you rub a slice of bread against the coarse side of the grater you make breadcrumbs.

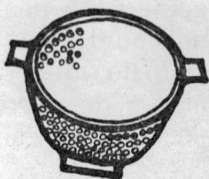

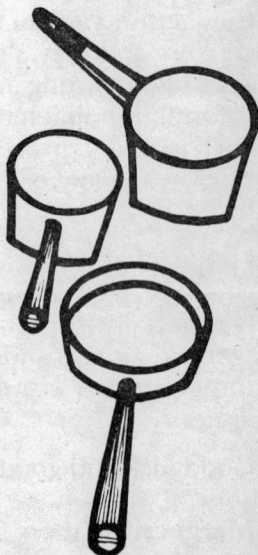

8

**Knives:** you will use several different kinds of knives when you cook. You will need a sharp knife for cutting and chopping. *Always be very careful how you use a sharp knife*. Ask a grown-up to help you chop difficult things. If you have a chopping board, cut on this so that you do not mark the table. Cut bread with a bread knife on a bread or chopping board. Spread butter on bread with a flat-bladed knife; a pointed knife makes holes in the bread. Lift food out of pans with a wide-bladed knife called a palette knife, or use a fish slice that looks like this.

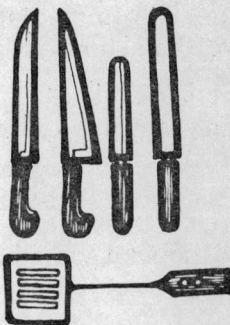

**Measures:** if you have a proper measuring jug use this; if not, remember that a teacup holds about 142 ml/¼ pint (generally called 150 ml) and a breakfast cup about 284 ml/½ pint (generally called 300 ml, see page 19). Many recipes give spoon measures; always fill the spoon so it is *level*, not more. Metric spoon measures are given on page 21.

**A pastry brush:** is used for many things including greasing baking tins and dishes. Take about 1 teaspoon of margarine or fat, warm it until soft enough to spread. Brush it over the dish, or rub the unmelted fat over the tin or dish with a clean piece of greaseproof paper.

**Scales:** if you have no scales a grown-up will help you work out the amounts. Today some people use metric

measures (grammes and kilogrammes), others use Imperial measures (ounces and pounds). This book gives you both: metric measures come first and Imperial follow in brackets immediately afterwards, so you can choose which to follow.

**Serving dishes:** sometimes the recipe just says use a serving dish, which means any kind of dish from the cupboard. In other recipes you are told to use an oven-proof dish: this means it is made of something like Pyrex which can be put into the oven but must not go on top of the cooker or under the grill. In other recipes you are told to use a heat-proof (some books call it a flame-proof) dish; this means the kind of special dish like Corning Ware or other heat-proof ware that can go under the grill or in the oven or on top of the cooker with complete safety.

**Sieves:** for straining liquids. Use small ones for tea or coffee, and larger ones where there is more liquid. You also need a sieve to make sure there are no lumps in flour or icing sugar or cocoa.

**Spoons:** when you stir use a wooden spoon, but when you measure use the type of spoon mentioned in the recipe.

**A whisk:** this is used to whip cream, beat up egg white, etc. There are various kinds: an electric whisk, see page 14, a rotary hand whisk, shown in the picture on the right, and a flat type of whisk.

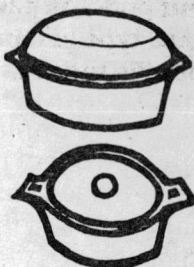

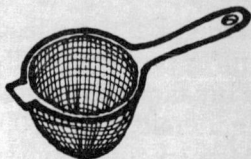

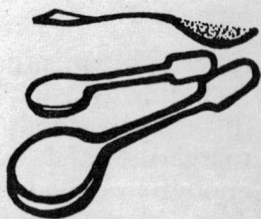

**A wok:** this is the name given to a conical pan as the picture on the right. The advantage of a wok as compared to an ordinary frying pan is that food cooks more rapidly and evenly. A wok can also be used instead of a saucepan, but the Chinese dish called sweet and sour pork, on page 112, is the most usual type of food associated with this cooking utensil.

# Words used in cooking

*Mixing*

**Beating:** means mixing the ingredients together with a very brisk movement. A wooden spoon is generally used when beating by hand.

**Blending:** also means mixing the ingredients together. Liquids are also blended together.

**Creaming:** means beating fat and sugar together until soft and fluffy; use a wooden spoon when creaming and stand the bowl on a folded teacloth so it does not slip.

**Folding:** is a turning movement done gently and slowly with a metal spoon, as in the Orange alaska (pages 165–6).

**Kneading:** means mixing the ingredients firmly together with your hands, as in home-made bread, rolls and buns (pages 119–33).

**Rubbing in:** is a method of mixing fat with flour with the tips of your fingers; you do this when making the pastry for the cherry tarts (pages 148–9).

**Whisking:** is a very brisk movement to whip cream or egg whites and is done with a whisk, see pages 156 and 165–6.

## Cooking

**Baking:** is a method of cooking food, such as cakes, in the oven.

**Boiling:** is cooking in liquid at boiling point (100°C or 212°F). The water for cooking vegetables is boiled (page 104, stage 27).

**Frying:** is cooking in fat. *Do be careful when you do this.* Page 77 tells you about testing the temperature of the fat.

**Grilling:** is cooking under the grill in a quick heat.

**Poaching:** is cooking food in liquid, which should simmer and not boil, see poached eggs on pages 54–5.

**Roasting:** is cooking food (generally meat, poultry or vegetables) in the oven. Meat and poultry can be roasted on a turning spit (called a rotisserie).

**Simmering:** is steady cooking in liquid. You should see an occasional bubble on the surface of the liquid.

**Warming:** hot foods should be served on hot plates or dishes. Heat these on racks on the top of the cooker, in the warming compartment or in the oven set very low.

# Electrical appliances for food preparation

The following equipment helps in preparing food; perhaps you have one of these appliances in your kitchen. Always ask a grown-up to show you how to operate these machines:

**An electric mixer:** there are large electrical mixers like the first picture on the right, or smaller ones as shown in the second picture. The basic mixer will do many things including these:

**a** Cream and beat ingredients together. Use it for the cakes on page 134 and 140, see also page 12.

**b** Whisk eggs and sugar as in the recipe for ice cream on page 153 or egg whites for a meringue, see page 166. It also will whip cream, but take care it does not over-beat the cream.

**c** Knead a bread or biscuit dough, see pages 122 and 158.

**d** Rub fat into flour. Be careful when doing this for it is easy for the mixture to be over-handled.

*Note:* Never put your fingers or a knife in the machine when in operation.

Ask a grown-up to show you how to use any extra attachments.

**A liquidizer:** this is often known as a blender. It will do many different things, including:

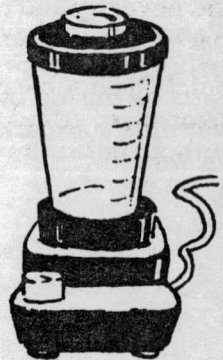

**a** Make a smooth purée of fruit or vegetables. It is used to make many soups.

**b** Make fine breadcrumbs and stuffings made from breadcrumbs and herbs. It will chop herbs.

**c** Make milk shakes (see *The Piccolo Cookbook*). The drinks given on pages 93 and 94 can be blended in the liquidizer.

*Note:* Never put a knife or your fingers into the liquidizer goblet when it is operating and *always* place the lid in position before switching on the machine.

**A food processor:** this does many of the jobs done by a liquidizer. In addition you can use a food processor for speedy creaming of ingredients, for slicing and chopping vegetables, see the picture right.

Ask an adult to show you how to lock the lid of the food processor in position and never try and remove this while the machine is in operation.

*Note!* The double cutting knife has razor sharp edges, so never handle this without an adult being present.

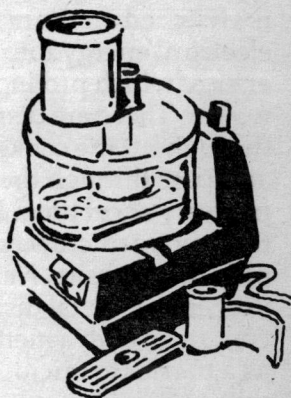

# Electrical appliances for cooking

In addition to a gas, solid fuel or electric cooker there are other appliances you may have in your home. Use these carefully under the guidance of an adult.

**An electric casserole:** this cooks stews and other foods very slowly. It looks like a large ordinary casserole. The Bolognese sauce on pages 85–9 can be cooked in the casserole.

**A sandwich toaster:** the toaster enables you to make a great variety of quick snacks. You will find suggestions on page 56 and in *The Piccolo Cookbook*.

**A microwave cooker:** when the cooker is switched on the magnetron converts electrical energy into microwave energy which produces invisible waves. These are distributed throughout the cooker by the stirrer and pass through the food, cooking it in a very short time. In some recipes in this book a microwave can be used, see page 17 opposite. *Never* use metal saucepans, metal dishes or any container with a metal rim. Metal acts as a barrier to microwaves so the food will not cook.

# Symbols used in this book

This means you will need to light the gas oven or switch on the electric oven. Your mother may prefer to do this for you. If you have a solid fuel oven ask a grown-up how to use it.

This symbol is for the grill, and shows that you will need to use it.

This shows that you use the top of the cooker. Check with an adult as to how you reduce the heat of a gas burner or electric hotplate during cooking.

This means you need to weigh the food on scales. This book gives both metric weights (grammes and kilos) and Imperial weights (ounces and pounds), see pages 18 and 19.

This is the symbol used to show there are directions for using a microwave cooker. Many foods can be placed in a microwave cooker. It is useful for speedy defrosting and for reheating food.

# The metric system

In Britain we have always used Imperial weights and measures, but nowadays much of the food we buy is sold with metric weights and measures. Equipment, such as cake tins, is also marked with metric measures. It is therefore important to know about Imperial *and* metric measurements. In recipes you will find that both are given. If one tries to give the exact Imperial measure it is often a very complicated amount. This is why you will find that in this, and many other books, an approximate weight or measure is suggested.

| Imperial weight | Metric weight | |
| --- | --- | --- |
| | Exact | Approx. |
| | grammes and kilogrammes | |
| 1 oz | 28.35 | 25 |
| 2 oz | 56.7 | 50 |
| 3 oz | 85.05 | 75 |
| 4 oz | 113.4 | 100 |
| 8 oz | 226.8 | 225 |
| 1 lb | 453.6 | or 0.5 kilo-grammes (kg) poor weight |
| 2 lb | 907.2 | or 1.00 kilo-gramme (kg) poor weight |

As you will see, the approximate amount is less than the real amount, so that you will produce slightly less mixture with the metric weights than with the Imperial ones.

# Measures

In recipes the exact millilitre measure is given to remind you to use as near this amount as possible; however your measure will show the approximate millilitre amount.

| Imperial measures | Metric measures | |
| --- | --- | --- |
| | Exact | Approx |
| | | millilitres (ml) |
| ¼ pint | 142 | 150 |
| ½ pint | 284 | 300 |
| ¾ pint | 426 | 450 |
| 1 pint | 568 | 600 |
| 1¼ pints | 710 | 750 |
| 1½ pints | 852 | 900 |
| 1¾ pints | 994 | 1000 ml or 1 litre* |
| 2 pints | 1136 | 1200 ml or 1.200 litres |

* 1 litre = 1.76 pints

| Imperial length | Metric length | |
| --- | --- | --- |
| | Exact | Approx |
| | | centimetres (cm) |
| 1 inch | 2.54 | 2.5 |
| 2 inches | 5.08 | 5 |
| 4 inches | 10.16 | 10 |
| 6 inches | 15.24 | 15 |
| 8 inches | 20.32 | 20 |
| 10 inches | 25.40 | 25 |

# Oven settings

In newer electric cookers oven temperatures will be in Celcius (°C) instead of Fahrenheit (°F). In recipes both these temperatures are given.

| Imperial temperature | | Metric temperature | |
| --- | --- | --- | --- |
| °F | Exact °C | Approx °C | |
| 200 | 93 | 90 |
| 225 | 107 | 110 |
| 250 | 121 | 130 |
| 275 | 135 | 140 |
| 300 | 149 | 150 |
| 325 | 163 | 160 or 170* |
| 350 | 177 | 180 |
| 375 | 190 | 190 |
| 400 | 204 | 200 |
| 425 | 218 | 220 |
| 450 | 232 | 230 |
| 475 | 246 | 240 |

The comparable setting for a gas cooker is given in the recipes.

* When Celcius temperatures were first used 170°C was given as the equivalent of 325°F but nowadays 160°C is more usual.

# Spoon measures

When measuring with a teaspoon or
tablespoon check that these are the
standard size. Below are the equivalent
metric spoon measures.

| Imperial spoon | Metric spoon |
| --- | --- |
| ½ teaspoon | 1 x 2.5 ml spoon |
| 1 teaspoon | 1 x 5 ml spoon |
| ½ tablespoon | 1 x 7.5 ml spoon |
| 1 tablespoon | 1 x 15 ml spoon |

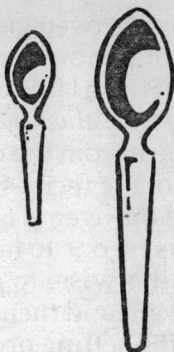

# Safety first

When you are cooking you will be
handling hot food and very hot pans, as
well as putting food into a heated oven
or removing hot dishes from the oven.

You also will be chopping, cutting and
doing other jobs that could cause
accidents if you are not careful. Here
are some of the things you should
remember:

*Always* keep saucepan or frying-pan
handles turned towards the middle of
the cooker for, if they stick out, you or
someone else could knock against the
handle and tip the pan over. When you
remove pans from the cooker, take care
they do not harm working surfaces: put
them on a mat or pan stand.

*Always* let a pan containing hot fat cool
down before you move it from the top
of the cooker. And *never* lean over a pan
of hot fat in case some splashes on to
your face or hands.

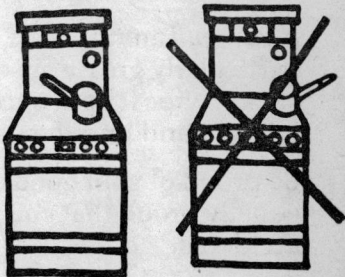

*Always* use oven gloves or a thick oven cloth for removing dishes from the oven. If it is a large or heavy dish, or if it is very hot, *always* ask a grown-up to remove it from the oven for you. None of the recipes in this book will spoil if the oven is not heated first so, if there is no one to help you with the oven, it is wiser to put the dish in the *cold* oven, and then light it or switch it on to the setting or temperature given in the recipe. But *never* do this unless you have been given permission by a grown-up and been shown exactly how to do it.

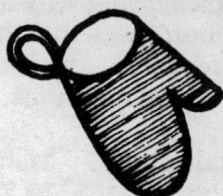

*Always* check that you have turned or switched off the heat from every part of the cooker when you have finished cooking.

*If anyone* does burn their hand on a hot dish put it in cold water *at once*, then tell a grown-up so they may see if it needs any treatment.

Young children must *never use sharp knives*; grown-ups will do most of the chopping for you, I am sure. Cut food on a chopping board so that you do not harm the working surfaces.

*If you spill* anything on the floor, particularly grease or something sticky, wipe it up at once so that no one will slip and hurt themselves.

Be proud of your good cooking and be equally proud that you do not cause accidents.

# Good shopping

I expect there are times when you shop for food. Here are some points to watch:

While waiting to be served work out just what you should pay for the food you buy, then you can check your change.

When you buy things in a supermarket check that food is carefully wrapped. Some foods are dated – bacon, for example. Make sure the date has not passed.

When you buy meat make sure it does not look dry and there is not *too much* fat; there should be *some* firm white fat on beef, firm cream fat on lamb or mutton and pinky-white fat on pork.

When you buy frozen foods carry them home as soon as possible so that they stay frozen. When you get home put them into the freezing part of the refrigerator or wrap them in newspaper to keep them frozen.

When you buy green vegetables make quite sure they look fresh; stale sprouts, cabbage or cauliflower have yellow leaves instead of fresh green leaves.

# Putting the food away

When you come home after shopping and are asked to unpack the food these are some of the things to remember.

Put ice cream or other frozen foods in the coolest place possible, that is, in the freezing compartment of the refrigerator or in the deep freeze or wrapped in newspaper in a cool cupboard.

Butter and other fats should be put into the special container in the refrigerator or into a cool cupboard.

Bread must be put into your special bread bin, drawer or other container. *Do not* store bread with crisp biscuits or pastry or cake. Each of these foods should be stored in separate containers.

Green vegetables should be taken out of their wrappings and put in a cool place; the more air they have the better they keep.

Fish and meat should be taken out of their wrappings, put on plates and placed in the refrigerator or the coolest part of the larder or ventilated cupboard.

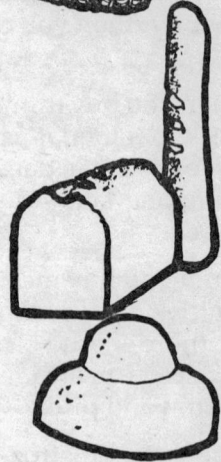

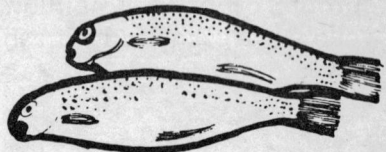

# The work of food

Most of us enjoy nice food and interesting dishes, but it is important that we also try to choose foods that are good for us, as well as being pleasant to eat.

Perhaps you do not know just what kinds of food are important to eat, so the following pages will tell you about some of these. On page 27 are suggestions for the kind of food we should try to eat every day. The names of some of the foods are below and on page 26 . Some foods provide more than one important nutrient (this word means 'nourishing ingredient'), for example meat has protein and fat as well as other important nutrients.

**Proteins** are found in all meat, chicken and other poultry, fish, cheese, eggs, milk, peas, beans and lentils and grains like wheat. Page 28 tells you about the work of proteins.

**Carbohydrates** is the name given to starch and sugar.

**Starch** is found in flour and anything made with flour (such as bread, cakes, spaghetti and other pasta). It is also in some vegetables like potatoes and peas. Pages 29 and 30 tell you more about this.

**Sugar** is found in sugar itself, in honey and treacle, and in anything made with sugar, like jam. Sugar is one of the foods that should be eaten in small quantities (see pages 29 and 30 ).

**Fats** are found in butter, margarine and other fats and oil, also in meat and some fish (like herrings). Page 32 tells you why you need some fat.

**Vitamins** are found in lots of food and pages 31 and 32 tell you more about them.

**Minerals** are found in many foods. Calcium and iron are two of the most important. Cheese is an excellent source of calcium. Calcium helps to maintain strong teeth and bones. Liver, heart, black treacle and spinach are rich in iron and this mineral is necessary for healthy blood.

**Fibre**: when the term 'fibre' is used in connection with the things we eat it means a substance obtained from plant food, as distinct from animal foods. All cereals, fruits and vegetables contain some dietary fibre; bran, beans, peas and oatmeal have a particularly high content of this important ingredient. Page 27 tells you why we need fibre.

# Foods to eat each day

The circle shows the groups of food we should try to eat each day, together with the names of some of the different products from which we can choose, including foods high in fibre as outlined on page 26 . In addition most people will eat some kind of sugar and sweetening each day. Pages 25 and 28 tell you more about the work of the different foods.

The importance of enough fibre each day is stressed by experts, for foods high in fibre help to keep us slim and prevent some serious illnesses.

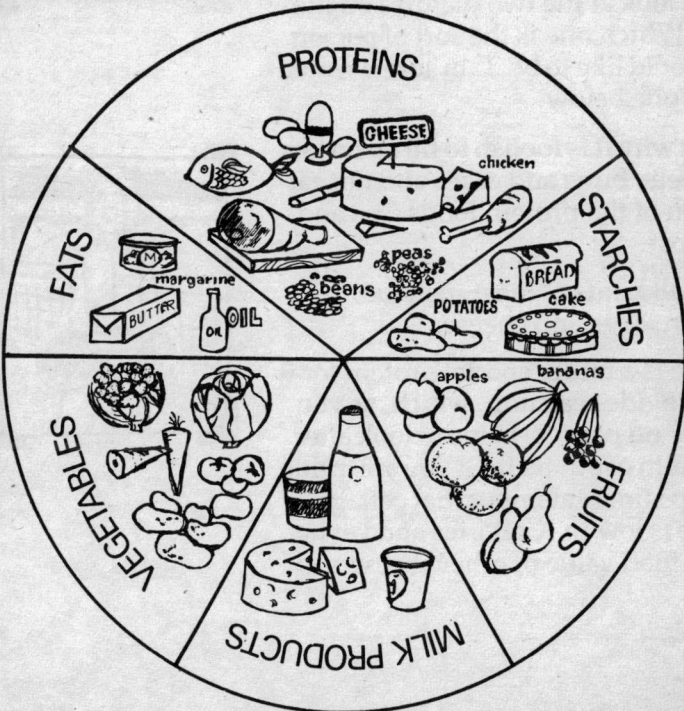

# How to be strong and healthy

Most of us want to be really strong and healthy and the foods we call proteins help us a great deal in this.

When you are young and growing you *must* have proteins to build strong bones and bodies. When you have finished growing you still *need* proteins to keep you strong and healthy.

In addition you need a good balance of other foods that provide vitamins, minerals and fibre (see pages 25 and 26).

Take a look at the two pictures on the right. Which one is the sort of person you would like to be: I am sure it would be the one below.

This is why it is foolish to fill up on lots of sweets, buns and cakes and not eat enough of the protein foods first and foremost.

Enjoy all kinds of meat, fish too, chicken, eggs and cheese.

Cheese is a rather special protein for it also provides calcium, which, as you will see on page 30 helps to look after the health of our teeth. If you are trying to keep slim remember that cottage cheese is low in K calories and yet has all the food value of other cheese.

# How to be slim

Often children and grown-ups are over-weight because they eat the *wrong* foods, *not* because they eat a lot of food.

Let us suppose you are rather fat. Perhaps it is because you do not take enough exercise, in which case you will soon slim down if you walk more or play more games. Perhaps it is because you are a *nibbler* or you eat too many starchy or sweet foods. Just think what you eat between meals. Do you have lots of buns, cakes, lollies, potato crisps, ice cream and fruit squash? This is probably the reason you are over-weight. So all you need to do is to *change* these rather bad habits. Eat an apple or a raw carrot or piece of celery between meals and notice the difference. Eat high-fibre foods as much as possible, for example choose wholemeal bread rather than white bread.

When it comes to meal times choose plates 3 and 4 instead of plates 1 and 2.

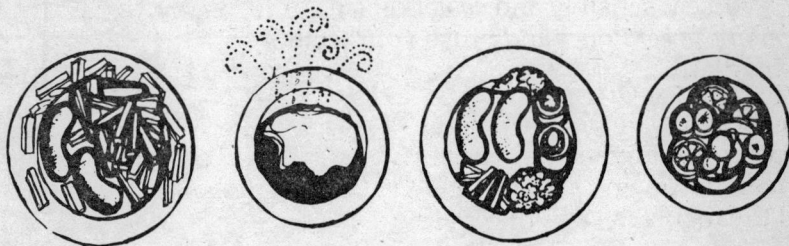

# How to have strong teeth

When people smile and show lovely strong white teeth it makes such a difference to their appearance, doesn't it? Many things help to give us good teeth:

Regular visits to the dentist.

Regular brushing.

If teeth are not brushed properly and regularly plaque forms and the acids in various foods (including apples and other fruit) affect the teeth adversely. If you brush your teeth correctly and frequently, plaque cannot form and then foods do not affect your teeth in the same way.

*Not too much sweet food or soft food:* we should give our teeth and gums plenty of work to do by eating crisp apples, celery, and other foods that need biting and crunching. Eat the right foods – and milk and cheese are the most important foods to help produce strong teeth.

If you eat sensibly and *do not eat too many sweet things* and brush your teeth regularly.

# How to have a clear skin

No one likes to have spots, do they? Often spots are just a sign of growing up and will soon vanish as you become older, particularly if you are careful to keep your skin very clean.

Sometimes spots appear because people eat the wrong foods. Too many sweets and too much fried food, like chips with most meals, help to produce spots.

There is a vitamin – known as vitamin C – that helps us to keep a clear skin, as well as shining hair and clear eyes.

Vitamin C is found in many fruits, particularly in fresh oranges and other citrus fruits, also strawberries and blackcurrants.

Vitamin C is also present in lots of vegetables, particularly green vegetables (they must be eaten raw or lightly cooked), potatoes (although potatoes are a starchy vegetable they also give us some vitamin C, particularly if you eat them when new and if you eat the skins) and tomatoes – and have these raw whenever possible.

Vitamin C is often called the protective vitamin, for in addition to looking after our skin, eyes and hair it is considered that it helps to build up resistance to infection.

# How to have lots of energy

Just think of all the things there are to do in a day. Our sketches show some of them.

In order to enjoy doing these things, as well as many others, you must have plenty of energy. Regular exercise and fresh air, the right amount of sleep and the right foods all help.

What are the right foods for energy?

We must have proteins – see pages 25, 27 and 28.

We need a certain amount of fat.

We need some starch, preferably in the form of bread, for this contains another important group of vitamins, called vitamin B group and they help so much to make us energetic.

We need a little sugar – but *not too much*.

We must have fruit, particularly those rich in vitamin C, see page 31.

Vegetables of all kinds are important, particularly those high in fibre, see page 26.

In other words, if you want to be really energetic you need a variety of foods; the recipes in this book will help to provide these in an interesting way.

# Snacks and quick supper dishes

The recipes on the following pages are suitable for supper and for lunchtime snacks (if you have a main meal at night), or they could form part of a substantial tea. There are several recipes that are ideal for packed meals too, on pages 81, 82 and 90.

The first recipes, on pages 34 to 40, are made with foods that you will find in most store cupboards. For example, sweet or savoury pancakes make a splendid snack.

The next snacks, on pages 41 to 74, are particularly quick; among snacks you will find milk drinks, for milk is a food as well as a beverage, see pages 93 and 94.

Perhaps you are planning to entertain some friends. You may enjoy making a quick supper dish or snack for them and you can find some rather more special recipes of this sort on pages 78 to 92.

Take time to make your snack look attractive; you can, for instance, garnish it with parsley or tomato, or as in the recipe.

It is interesting to learn about food from other countries; there are recipes on pages 79 to 92.

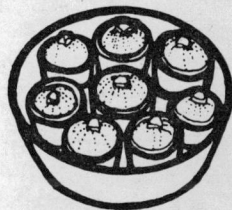

# Pancakes

Home-made pancakes can be served as a pudding or a savoury dish. The batter is very easy to make. Read the instructions on page 21 about the importance of looking after hot frying pans.

## Pancakes with lemon

**You will need:**

| | |
|---|---|
| flour (preferably plain) | 100 grammes (4 oz) |
| salt | pinch |
| egg | 1 |
| milk or a mixture of milk and water | 250 ml *(1/2 pint) |

for frying:

| | |
|---|---|
| fat | 50 grammes (2oz)† see page 35 |

for serving:

| | |
|---|---|
| caster sugar | 25 grammes (1 oz) |
| lemon | 1 |

*These ingredients will make 8 pancakes.*

**You will use:**
plates for ingredients, sieve, large basin, cup or small basin, measuring jug, wooden spoon or whisk, 18–20 cm (7–8 inch) frying pan, flat knife, jug, palette knife or fish slice, oven-proof serving plate, greaseproof paper, sharp knife, chopping board, sugar dredger.

* use this metrication
† Make sure the fat is really hot before cooking each pancake. If using a special pancake pan you may find you need less fat.

**For success:**
Whisk the pancake batter just before cooking.

Pour only a very little batter into the pan so you have thin pancakes.

**1** If you want to keep the pancakes hot in the oven set this to very slow, 275°F, 140°C or gas mark 1. To keep them hot on top of the cooker half fill a large saucepan with water and heat it.

**2** Sieve the flour and salt into a large basin.

**3** Break the egg into a cup or small basin and pour it into the flour.

**4** Add about ¼ of the milk or milk and water and stir carefully with a wooden spoon until the flour is blended with the egg and milk.

**5** Beat really hard with the wooden spoon until you have a thick smooth mixture. It is now called a thick batter. This batter could be made in a food processor or liquidizer, see pages 14 and 15.

**6** Some people like to let the thick batter stand before adding the rest of the liquid; others add the liquid straight away. Whichever method you use, pour the rest of the liquid into the thick batter very slowly, beating all the time so that it does not become lumpy. You may then like to change the wooden spoon for a whisk as it is important that the batter is light. When you've beaten enough, bubbles should rise to the top of the mixture. When all

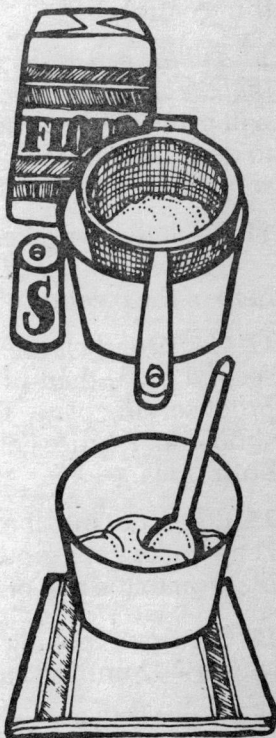

the liquid has been added, let the batter stand in a cool place until you are ready to use it.

**7** Light the gas burner or switch on the electric hotplate.

**8** Divide the fat into 8 pieces. Put one piece into the frying pan, heat steadily until melted. You will need 1 piece of fat for cooking each pancake, or see page 35.

**9** Transfer the batter to a jug and pour enough into the hot fat to give a very thin coating.

**10** *Tilt the pan as shown in the picture so that the batter runs evenly over the pan.* It will probably be better for a grown-up to do this first to show you the best way.

**11** Cook the pancake for 2 minutes over a medium heat, then turn with the help of the palette knife or fish slice.

**12** Cook for the same time on the second side, then lift on to the oven-proof serving plate. The pancake should look a nice golden brown on both sides.

**13** Either put into the very cool oven to keep hot or get a grown-up to lift the plate on to the pan of very hot water.

**14** Continue cooking the pancakes as stages 7-12 until all are ready.

**15** Sprinkle the sugar over the greaseproof paper.

**16** Take the pancakes off the plate and roll neatly on the sugared paper. Be careful not to burn your fingers as you do this for they are very hot.

**17** Cut the lemon into slices.

**18** Lift the pancakes back on to the serving plate and serve with slices of lemon.

*Note!* If you are having an informal meal, make one pancake and serve it at once, rolled up, with sugar and lemon. Make the second pancake and continue like this. It saves all the bother of keeping the pancakes hot.

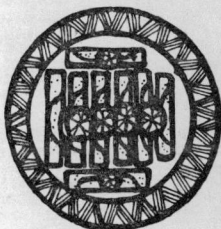

# Tomato pancakes

**1** You will use the same mixture for the pancakes as page 34 and cook them in the same way. You will not need the sugar or lemon.

It is a good idea to prepare the tomato filling *before* cooking the pancakes.

**You will need:**

| | |
|---|---|
| *bacon* | 3 rashers |
| *tomatoes* | small can |
| *salt* | very small pinch |
| *pepper* | shake |

to garnish:
*parsley*              small sprig

**2** Cut away the bacon rinds and chop the bacon into small pieces with kitchen scissors or a sharp knife on a chopping board.

**3** Light the gas burner or switch on the electric hotplate.

**4** Put the bacon rinds and the pieces of bacon into a small saucepan or frying pan and fry for 3 minutes.

**5** Take the pan off the heat and lift out the bacon rinds. (You added these to give more fat; you can discard them now.)

**6** Open the can of tomatoes, or ask a grown-up to do this for you, and tip the tomatoes and the liquid from the can into the saucepan with the bacon. Chop the tomatoes into smaller pieces with a knife and fork. You can do this in the saucepan.

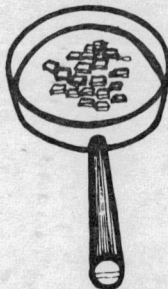

**7** Add a very small pinch of salt, because most bacon is fairly salty anyway, and a shake of pepper.

**8** Put the tomato mixture back on top of the cooker but do not heat again until nearly all the pancakes are cooked.

**9** Cook the pancakes as instructed on pages 34–7 and keep them hot.

**10** Heat the tomato mixture for a few minutes only.

**11** Put the first pancake on to a hot serving dish, top with some of the tomato mixture, then add a second pancake, more tomato mixture and continue like this until you have used all the pancakes and all the tomato mixture.

**12** Top with the parsley. To serve, cut these pancakes into slices, like a cake.

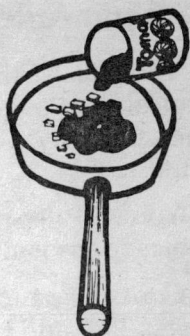

# Jam pancakes

1 You will use the same mixture for the pancakes as page 34 and cook these in the same way; you will not need the lemon.

2 You will also need about 4–6 tablespoons jam.

3 Cook the pancakes as directed on pages 35–7 and keep them hot.

4 Put the jam into a saucepan.

5 Light the gas burner or switch on the electric hotplate; set to a very low heat.

6 Heat the jam for 2–3 minutes only, then take it off the heat.

7 Tip the first pancake on to the sugared paper, spread with a little warm jam and roll up neatly.

8 Do the same thing with all the pancakes and serve at once.

## To make a change

Fill the pancakes with cold raw fruit or heated cooked or canned fruit.

**Fruit pancakes.** Fill the hot pancakes with hot thick fruit or heated canned or cooked fruit or with cold sliced strawberries or other ripe fruit or with fruit-flavoured yogurt.

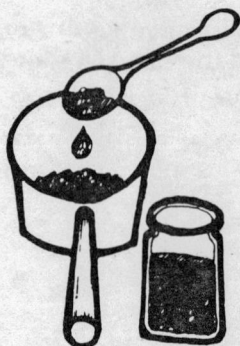

# Eggs mornay

When you read the word 'mornay' you will know the food is served with a cheese sauce. This recipe makes a very good supper dish. Make sure you use a dish that can be put under the grill to brown. Incidentally, when the mixture is browned, it is called *au gratin*.

**You will need:**

| eggs | 4 |
|------|---|

for the sauce:

| | |
|---|---|
| cheese | 50 grammes (2 oz) |
| flour | 25 grammes (1 oz) |
| salt | pinch |
| pepper | shake |
| milk | 284 ml (½ pint) |
| butter or margarine | 25 grammes (1 oz) |

for the topping:

| | |
|---|---|
| grated cheese | 25 grammes (1 oz) |
| breadcrumbs | 2 tablespoons |

to garnish:

| | |
|---|---|
| tomatoes | 2 |

*These ingredients will make 4 servings.*

**You will use:**
plates for ingredients, 2 saucepans, 2 basins, tablespoon, grater, wooden spoon, measuring jug, knife, heat-proof serving dish, chopping board.

**For success:**
Stir the sauce carefully at stage 13 so it keeps smooth.

Do not cook the sauce when you have put in the cheese, otherwise the mixture becomes 'lumpy' – the proper word for this is 'curdling'.

1 Put enough cold water into a saucepan to cover the eggs.

2 Carry the eggs to the cooker in a basin. Lower them into the cold water with a tablespoon and put the saucepan over the burner or hotplate.

3 Light the gas burner or switch on the electric hotplate.

4 Bring the egg water to the boil, then adjust the heat so that it isn't bubbling too fiercely. Look at your watch or a clock and allow the eggs to boil for 10 minutes – no longer.

5 Lift the eggs out of the water and put them into a basin of cold water.

6 When you can touch the eggs, lift them out and crack the shells; this makes sure the eggs cool quickly.

7 While the eggs are boiling you can start to prepare the sauce.

8 Grate the cheese on to a plate; you can also grate the cheese for the topping and put this on to a second plate. You are now ready to make the sauce.

9 *Blending method:* Mix the flour with the salt and pepper in a basin.

10 Gradually add a quarter of the cold milk, stirring with a wooden spoon until you have a smooth paste.

**11** Put the rest of the milk into a saucepan and bring this to boiling point. Take care it does not boil over.

**12** Pour the boiling milk slowly over the flour mixture, stirring all the time to prevent lumps forming.

**13** Tip the sauce back into the pan and put over a *low* heat. Stir until the mixture boils. Then continue boiling for 3 minutes, stirring all the time. Add the butter or margarine.

**14** When stirring the sauce, make sure that the wooden spoon scrapes across the bottom and into the corners of the pan. If the sauce becomes a little lumpy, remove the pan from the heat, beat the sauce with the wooden spoon, or better still with a hand whisk, until it becomes smooth. There is another way to make the sauce, see under *Note*.

**15** Add the cheese, stir to melt the cheese but do not cook the sauce again.

**16** Take the shells off the eggs, put the shelled eggs on to a plate and cut them into halves then place into the heat-proof dish with the white side uppermost.

**17** Light the gas grill or switch on the electric grill.

**18** Pour the hot cheese sauce over the eggs.

**19** Sprinkle the grated cheese and breadcrumbs over the top of the sauce.

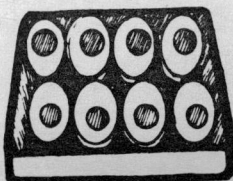

**20** Carry to the cooker and put under the grill; cook for about 4 minutes, until the top is really brown and crisp.

**21** Lift the dish from under the grill very carefully. You will need oven gloves.

**22** Cut the two tomatoes into halves and put on top of the dish and serve at once.

A cheese sauce can be used in many ways. *The Piccolo Cookbook* gives you two recipes using this, see pages 68–73.

*Note! One-stage sauce:* If you have soft (luxury) margarine you can put this into the saucepan with the 25 grammes (1 oz) flour and 284 ml (½ pint) milk then heat the sauce steadily, whisking all the time until thickened. After this add a little salt and pepper and proceed as stage 15 onwards.

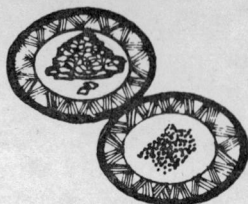

## To make a change

**Poached eggs mornay.** Instead of the hard-boiled eggs in this dish or in eggs florentine, you can use poached eggs instead.

**Fish mornay.** Instead of using cooked eggs in this dish or in eggs florentine, use lightly cooked portions of white fish. It is a good way of using leftover fish.

If you have any cooked spinach left you can put this in the dish at stage 16 and lay the halved eggs on top. The recipe is then called **eggs florentine.**

# Tulip cups

These are like small tarts but save you the trouble of making pastry for they are made with thin slices of bread. In this recipe the crisp shapes are filled with heated baked beans. There are many other suggestions for savoury fillings on page 48, or you could choose a sweet filling and serve the tulip cups as a dessert or for tea.

**You will need:**

| | |
|---|---|
| *bread* | 8-9 thin slices from a small fresh loaf |
| *butter* or *margarine* | 40 grammes (1½ oz) |
| *baked beans* | medium can |

*These ingredients will make 8-9 cups.*

**You will use:**
bread knife, bread board (unless using ready sliced bread), plate, rolling pin, flat-bladed knife, patty (bun) tins, can opener, saucepan, wooden spoon, serving plate, tablespoon.

**For success:**
Use fresh bread and roll it at stage 4.

Make sure the oven is really hot.

**1** Set your oven to moderately hot to hot, 400-425°F, 200-220°C or gas mark 6-7.

**2** Slice the bead (unless using ready sliced bread) or ask a grown-up to do this for you; there is no need to cut off the crusts.

**3** Put the butter or margarine on a plate and leave it in a warm place to soften slightly – do not melt it.

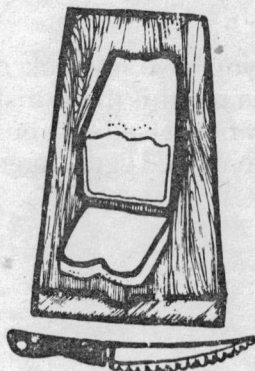

**4** Roll the bread with the rolling pin on a dry working surface. This makes it easy to handle and it will not break when put into the patty (bun) tins.

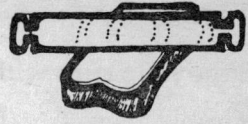

**5** Spread one side of the bread with half the butter or margarine.

**6** Press the greased side of the bread into the patty (bun) tins to get a shape as shown in the picture.

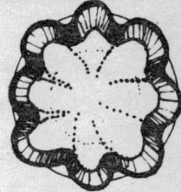

**7** Spread inside the bread shapes with the rest of the butter or margarine.

**8** Bake for 10 minutes towards the top of a moderately hot to hot oven until crisp and golden brown.

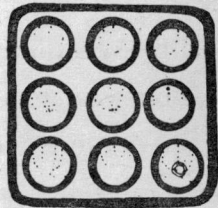

**9** Meanwhile, open the can of beans or ask a grown-up to do this for you.

**10** Tip the beans and sauce from the can into the saucepan.

**11** Light the gas burner or switch on the electric hotplate.

**12** Heat the beans gently for a few minutes, stir with a wooden spoon so they do not burn as they heat.

**13** Take the tulip cups out of the oven, lift them very carefully out of the patty (bun) tins and put them on the serving plate.

**14** Fill each cup shape with the hot beans and serve at once.

## To make a change

Fill the tulip cups with:

Scrambled eggs (see **The Piccolo Cookbook,** pages 50–51 and pages 52–3 in this book).

Cheese sauce (see pages 41–5) mixed with cooked vegetables.

Mashed sardines and slices of tomato.

Cooked tomatoes topped with grated cheese.

Or with sweet fillings:

Jam, honey, marmalade or lemon curd.

Cooked or canned fruit, well drained.

Let the tulip cups get cold and fill with ice cream and decorate with grated chocolate.

# Snacks on toast

These are very quick to prepare. **The Piccolo Cookbook** gives you some suggestions, and here (up to page 56) are some more.

Toast 4 slices of bread, spread with butter or margarine, then spread with one of the following:

(*All quantities will cover the 4 slices.*)

**Cheese and ham.** Blend 100 grammes (4oz) cream cheese with 50 grammes (2oz) chopped cooked ham and 1 tablespoon chutney. Serve at once.

**Curried eggs.** Hard-boil 4 eggs, shell and chop, then mix with 2 tablespoons mayonnaise and ½–1 teaspoon curry powder. Serve at once.

**Date and cheese.** Blend 100 grammes (4 oz) grated Cheddar cheese, 2 tablespoons milk and 50 grammes (2 oz) chopped cooking dates. Serve at once.

**Toasted cheese and baked beans.** Heat a medium can of baked beans. Spoon on top of the hot buttered toast. Cover each serving of toast and beans with a slice of processed cheese. Put under the grill for about 1 minute, until the cheese starts to melt. Serve at once.

# Bengal toasts

This is really an Indian type of recipe, for it mixes curry powder and chutney with the ham, which makes it very tasty. You can use canned ham if you like.

**You will need:**

| | |
|---|---|
| *bread* | 4 slices |
| *butter or margarine* | 40 grammes (1½ oz) |
| *cooked ham* | 100 grammes (4 oz) |
| *chutney* | 1 tablespoon |
| *curry powder* | ½-1 *level* teaspoon |

to garnish:

| | |
|---|---|
| *tomatoes* | 2 |

*These ingredients will make 4 servings.*

**You will use:**
plates for ingredients, basin, sharp knife, chopping board, fork, tablespoon, teaspoon, flat-bladed knife, serving plates.

**For success:**
Cut the ham into very small pieces so you can mix it with the chutney and other things.

**1** Light the gas grill or switch on the electric grill and put the bread on to the top (called the grid) of the grill pan. Do not toast it until you have made the ham mixture.

**2** Put half the butter or margarine into a basin.

**3** Cut the ham into small pieces on the board, then tip it into the basin.

**4** Mash it with the butter or margarine, then add the chutney and curry powder.

**5** Toast the bread on both sides, spread with the rest of the butter or margarine, then with the ham mixture.

**6** Put back under the grill and heat for 1 minute only.

**7** Cut each tomato across the middle.

**8** Lift the Bengal toasts on to the warmed serving plates and put a tomato half on top of each serving.

## Bengal cheese toasts

**1** Follow the recipe for Bengal toasts page 50 up to the end of stage 5.

**2** Sprinkle each serving with 1 tablespoon finely grated Cheddar cheese, then continue as stage 6 but allow about 2 minutes under the grill.

**3** Continue as stages 7 and 8.

# Scrambled eggs

The method of scrambling eggs is given in detail in **The Piccolo Cookbook**, pages 50–51. The amounts given below make generous sized portions for 2 people.

**1** Choose 3–4 eggs, 40 grammes (1½oz) butter or margarine and 2 large slices of bread. Toast the bread, spread with some of the butter or margarine and keep hot.

**2** Beat the eggs with 2 tablespoons milk and a little salt and pepper.

**3** Heat the remaining butter or margarine in a saucepan, add the eggs and cook *slowly*, stir gently with a wooden spoon when the eggs start to set. Do not over-stir.

**4** Continue cooking, stirring occasionally, until the eggs are like thick cream. Spoon on to the toast and serve.

*Note!* If preferred the eggs can be scrambled in a microwave cooker; beat these as stage 2. Place the butter or margarine in an oven-proof dish or basin and heat, add the eggs and cook. Stir once or twice with a wooden spoon during cooking.

## To make a change

**Cheesey eggs.** The ingredients are the same as for scrambled eggs. Add 2–3 tablespoons grated cheese at the end of stage 3.

Instead of cheese you could add a little chopped ham or chicken or cooked vegetables.

## Atlantic eggs

**1** Ingredients as scrambled eggs on page 52 (method is given in greater detail in **The Piccolo Cookbook**). If using canned fish, which is highly salted, be sparing with the salt you add.

**2** Open a small can of tuna fish, pink salmon, shrimps or prawns, or use any cooked smoked fish (haddock, cod or kippers) that might have been leftover. *Always be careful when using up leftover fish* as stale food can cause poisoning and fish is particularly likely to do this. Drain canned fish if rather salty in flavour.

**3** Remove any skin and bones from the fish, then flake or chop it; do not use the liquid from canned fish in this recipe.

**4** Heat the butter or margarine in the saucepan, add the fish, then the beaten eggs and proceed to scramble the mixture. Serve on hot buttered toast.

# Poached eggs

There are 3 ways of poaching eggs. Toast the bread, spread this with a little butter or margarine and keep it hot while poaching the eggs.

## Method 1: using an egg poacher

**1** Put a knob of butter about the size of a small nut (i.e. 7 grammes (¼ oz)) into each metal cup required (allow 1 or 2 eggs per person).

**2** Place the metal cups in the rack and stand this over the pan which should be half filled with cold water.

**3** Put the pan over a moderate heat and leave until the water in the pan is simmering and the butter or margarine has melted.

**4** Meanwhile crack the shell of the first egg; break the egg into a cup and then slide this into the metal cup. Repeat this with the rest of the eggs.

**5** Cover the poacher with the lid and allow the water to boil steadily for about 3½ minutes or until the eggs are set.

**6** Turn off the heat, then lift the first metal cup from the water – *use oven gloves for this* – or ask a grown-up to do it for you. Slide the egg on to the toast.

## Method 2: using small basins or old cups

Put the butter or margarine into the basins or cups as stage 1 on page 54. Stand these in a saucepan half filled with cold water. Bring the water to simmering point as stage 3 on page 54. Break the egg into an ordinary cup, then slide this into the hot basin or cup as stage 4 on page 54. Do this with all the eggs then cover the saucepan and proceed as stages 5 and 6 on page 54.

## Method 3: poaching the eggs in water

**1** Bring about 284 ml (½ pint) water to boiling point in a shallow saucepan or deep frying pan. Add a pinch of salt to the water plus ½ teaspoon vinegar (this is not essential, but it does help to prevent the egg whites from spreading).

**2** Break the egg into a cup as stage 4 on page 54, then slide it into the hot water. Continue like this with the other eggs.

**3** Allow the water to simmer steadily for 3 minutes or until the eggs are set.

**4** Lift the eggs from the water with a perforated spoon or fish slice and serve them.

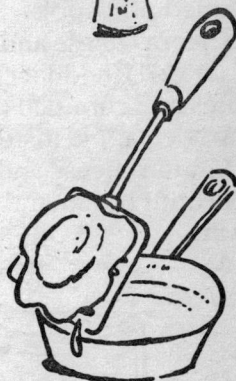

# Toasted sandwiches

In **The Piccolo Cookbook** are suggestions for easy toasted sandwiches (see pages 39–40). These sandwiches can be quickly made with the help of a grill or electric toaster.

Always pre-heat the grill or electric toaster before toasting the sandwiches. Make the sandwiches in the usual way by spreading slices of bread with butter or margarine then sandwiching 2 slices with the filling.

If using a grill, toast the sandwiches on one side, then turn them over and toast on the second side.

If using a sandwich toaster, you will find both sides of the bread are toasted simultaneously.

Here are some interesting fillings:

**a** Baked beans and grated cheese.
**b** Cottage cheese and well-drained canned pineapple.
**c** Cream cheese and grated carrot.
**d** Grated Cheddar cheese and chopped dates and chopped nuts, or use chopped apple instead of dates.
**e** Grated cheese and chutney.
**f** Peanut butter and cooked bacon or ham.

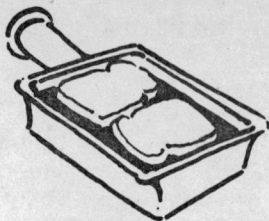

# Fish twists

**You will need:**

*fish fingers*      8
*streaky bacon*      4 rashers

*These ingredients make 4 large portions.*

**You will use:**
chopping board, kitchen scissors or sharp knife, 8 wooden cocktail sticks, fish slice, serving dish.

**For success:**

**1** Light the gas grill or switch on the electric grill, heat thoroughly.

**2** Separate the fish fingers but do not allow them to defrost. Cut the rinds from the bacon, and cut each rasher lengthways so you have 8 strips.

**3** Wind these in a spiral (like the picture) round the fish fingers and put in the cocktail sticks to hold them together.

**4** Put them on to the rack (grid) of the grill pan; cook under the hot grill for 2 minutes. Turn over and grill quickly on the other side for 2 minutes.

**5** Lower the heat of the grill and finish cooking for 5–6 minutes.

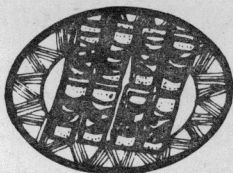

# Beef stuffed tomatoes

This is a good way of using a small piece of corned beef and some large tomatoes. You can also include some chives, which are a herb that looks like grass. Chives have a mild oniony flavour and are excellent in omelettes and salads.

**You will need:**

| | |
|---|---|
| *tomatoes* | 4 large |
| *corned beef* | about 75 grammes (3 oz)* |
| *chives* | 4–5 blades |
| *soft breadcrumbs* | 3 tablespoons |
| *salt* | pinch |
| *pepper* | shake |

for the topping:

| | |
|---|---|
| *soft breadcrumbs* | 1½ tablespoons |
| *margarine* | knob |

*These ingredients will make 4 small or 2 large servings.*

**You will use:**
plates for ingredients, chopping board, sharp knife, teaspoon, basin, fork, kitchen scissors, baking tin plus serving dishes or an oven-proof dish.

**For success:**
Do not over-cook the tomatoes.

**1** Set your oven to moderate, 375°F, 190°C or gas mark 5.

**2** Cut the tomatoes in halves across the middle; scoop out the centre pulp with a teaspoon and put it into a basin.

* Most cans of corned beef weigh about 350 grammes (12 oz); page 62 gives a recipe to use the rest of the beef.

**3** Chop the pulp with a knife and fork.

**4** Cut the corned beef into small pieces, tip into the basin containing the tomato pulp and mash well.

**5** Cut the chives into tiny pieces with kitchen scissors, add to the corned beef with the 3 tablespoons of breadcrumbs.

**6** Mix well with the fork, add the salt and pepper.

**7** Put the tomato cases on to a baking tin or into an oven-proof dish.

**8** Spoon the mixture into the tomato cases.

**9** Sprinkle with the breadcrumbs over the top and put a tiny piece of margarine, about the size of a pea, on top of each tomato half.

**10** Carry the dish carefully to the oven so that the tomato halves do not fall over.

**11** Bake for 10 minutes just above the centre of a moderate oven if you like very firm tomatoes, or 15 minutes if you like soft ones, then serve at once.

*Note!* To make a complete meal you could cook peas or heat baked beans on top of the cooker, to serve with the tomato dish.

## To make a change

**Cheese stuffed tomatoes.** Ingredients as the recipe but use 75 grammes (3 oz) grated cheese instead of corned beef.

**Egg stuffed tomatoes.** Ingredients as the recipe but use 2 large eggs instead of the corned beef. Break the eggs, beat lightly and add to the chopped tomato (stage 4) and continue as the recipe.

**Ham stuffed tomatoes.** Ingredients as the recipe but use 75 grammes (3 oz) cooked ham instead of corned beef. Chop the ham at stage 4. You could use chopped cooked tongue or beef or lamb or pork or chicken too.

# Stuffed tomato salad

Stuffed tomatoes make an excellent salad dish or they can be served as the first course of a meal.

**For success:**
Choose 4 really ripe large tomatoes.

**1** Halve the tomatoes, remove and chop the pulp as described on page 59 stages 2–3.

**2** Mix the chopped tomato pulp with *one* of the following fillings:

**a** 75 grammes (3 oz) cottage cheese, 1 tablespoon finely chopped parsley and 1–2 teaspoons chopped capers.

**b** 50 grammes (2 oz) diced Cheddar cheese.

**c** 2–3 shelled and chopped hard-boiled eggs.

**d** 75 grammes (3 oz) well-drained flaked cooked or canned fish of any kind.

**e** 75 grammes (3 oz) chopped corned beef or cooked meat.

**f** 50 grammes (2 oz) shelled and chopped prawns, 1 tablespoon peeled and finely diced cucumber and 1 tablespoon mayonnaise or salad dressing.

**3** Add salt and pepper to taste, put the filling into the tomato cases and serve on lettuce.

# Corned beef hamburgers

These are an excellent way in which to use corned beef. There are other hamburgers in **The Piccolo Cookbook** on pages 61–3.

**You will need:**

| | |
|---|---|
| *corned beef* | approx. 275 grammes (9 oz)* |
| *onion* | 1 small |
| *potato* | 1 medium |
| *salt* | pinch |
| *pepper* | shake |

for frying:
| | |
|---|---|
| *fat* | 50 grammes (2 oz) |

to garnish:
| | |
|---|---|
| *parsley or* | |
| *watercress* | small bunch |

*These ingredients will make 4 large or 6 smaller hamburgers.*

**You will use:**
plates for ingredients, sharp knife, chopping board, basin, fork, potato peeler or small vegetable knife, grater, flat knife, frying pan, fish slice, serving dish.

**For success:**
Press the beef mixture well at stage 6 so that the hamburgers keep a firm shape. Turn carefully at stage 10.

**1** Cut the corned beef into small pieces, then tip into the basin and mash with a fork; this is quite easy to do.

* Most cans of corned beef weigh about 350 grammes (12 oz); page 58 gives a recipe to use the rest of the beef.

**2** Peel the onion and the potato, keep the potato in a basin of water or covered with foil until you are ready to grate it, as it turns a black colour very easily. If you have put the potato into water dry it well before grating it.

**3** Rub the onion and then the potato against the coarse side of the grater, and allow the grated pieces of vegetable to drop into the basin containing the corned beef.

**4** Mix the beef with the grated onion, potato, salt and pepper.

**5** Take the mixture out of the basin and divide into 4 or 6 portions.

**6** Pat each portion into a neat round cake.

**7** Put the fat into a frying pan and put this on to the cooker.

**8** Light the gas burner or switch on the electric hotplate.

**9** Heat the fat until it has melted. *Do not have the heat too high*.

**10** Put in the hamburgers and cook for 3 minutes on one side. Turn over one hamburger; if this looks light brown on the one side, you have cooked the meat cakes for sufficiently long on that side, so turn over all the other hamburgers. You will find it is easier to lift them with a fish slice than with a knife.

**11** Cook for 3 minutes on the second side. *Watch the heat carefully and turn it down* if you find the hamburgers are cooking too quickly.

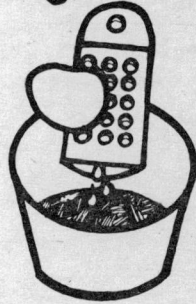

**12** Lift out of the pan on to a hot dish.
Arrange the washed parsley or
watercress round the hamburgers.

*Note!* To make a complete meal cook
cauliflower or another green vegetable
to serve with the hamburgers.

## To make a change

**Oatmeal burgers.** Omit the potato and
add 25 grammes (1 oz) rolled oats
instead.

# Cheeseburgers

**1** For this recipe you can make your own hamburgers, as described on pages 62 to 64 or you can use ready made frozen hamburgers. You will also need 4 tablespoons grated cheese.

**2** Cook the hamburgers as in the recipe or follow the instructions on the packet.

**3** When the hamburgers are cooked place them on an oven-proof serving dish, or put them on toasted rolls or slices of toast and then on the serving dish.

**4** Set your oven to moderate or moderately hot, 375–400°F, 190–200°C or gas mark 5–6.

**5** Sprinkle the grated cheese on top of the hamburgers, then put the dish into the oven for 5 minutes only, until the cheese has melted. Serve at once.

## To make a change

Put a ring of well-drained canned pineapple on top of the cooked hamburgers, then top with the cheese at stage 5.

Spread the hamburgers with tomato chutney or tomato ketchup, then top with the cheese at stage 5.

# Sardine crisp

This makes sardines into a more interesting snack.

**You will need:**

| | |
|---|---|
| *bread* | 4 slices |
| *sardines in oil* | 1 medium can |
| *Cheddar cheese* | 50 grammes (2 oz) |
| *breadcrumbs* | 2 tablespoons |
| *milk* | 2 tablespoons |
| *salt* | pinch |
| *pepper* | shake |

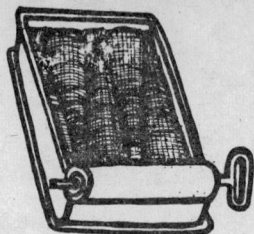

*These ingredients will make 4 servings.*

**You will use:**

plates for ingredients, bread knife and bread board (unless using sliced bread), basin, grater, tablespoon, flat-bladed knife, serving dish or 4 plates.

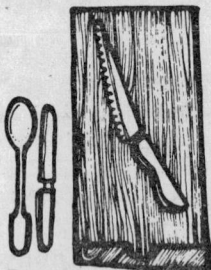

**For success:**

Have the grill really hot, so the cheese topping browns quickly.

**1** Light the gas grill or switch on the electric grill.

**2** Toast the bread on both sides.

**3** Open the can of sardines, or ask a grown-up to do this for you.

**4** Drain the oil from the can of sardines into the basin, then lift the sardines out and put them on to the hot toast (there is no need to spread the toast with butter or margarine).

**5** Grate the cheese and add to the sardine oil in the basin.

**6** Mix in the breadcrumbs and milk, then the salt and pepper, stir with the knife.

**7** Spread the mixture on top of the sardines and heat for about 3 minutes under the grill.

**8** Lift off the grill pan on to the hot dish or plates and serve at once.

## To make a change

You could use this breadcrumb and cheese topping over:
**a** cooked tomatoes on toast.
**b** baked beans on toast.
**c** cooked mushrooms on toast.
As you would not have the oil from the sardines you would need to add 1 tablespoon of salad oil at stage 4.

It would not be as easy to spread the topping over the foods suggested above; you would just sprinkle it on, then brown it at stage 7.

# Salmon pie

This is a very delicious supper dish. You can use a packet of instant mashed potato instead of cooking fresh potatoes. Pink salmon is cheaper than red salmon, and very good in this recipe.

**You will need:**

for the potato topping:

| | |
|---|---|
| potatoes | 450 grammes (1 lb) |
| salt | ¼ level teaspoon |
| margarine | 25 grammes (1 oz) |
| milk | 2 tablespoons |
| pepper | shake |

for the salmon filling:

| | |
|---|---|
| pink salmon | 1 medium can |
| lemon | 1 |
| eggs | 2 |
| milk | 4 tablespoons |
| salt | pinch |
| pepper | shake |

to garnish:

| | |
|---|---|
| parsley | sprig |

*These ingredients will make 4 servings.*

**You will use:**
plates for ingredients, bowl, potato peeler or sharp knife, saucepan, sieve or colander, fork, potato masher, tablespoon, wooden spoon, can opener, basin, sharp knife, chopping board, lemon squeezer, cup, oven-proof serving dish, flat-bladed knife.

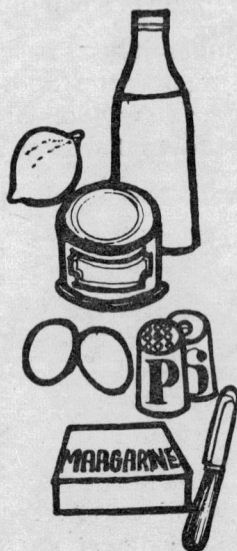

**For success:**
Cook the potatoes carefully, so you have a very smooth topping.

**1** Fill a bowl with cold water, so you can put the potatoes into this as you peel them; this saves them going black.

**2** Half fill the saucepan with water, add the salt, take to the cooker.

**3** Light the gas burner or switch on the electric hotplate.

**4** Bring the water to the boil, add the potatoes, cover the pan and turn down the heat, for potatoes should cook *steadily*.

**5** Test to see if the potatoes are soft after about 20 minutes; use the tip of a knife. If they are not quite ready let them go on cooking for a little longer.

**6** When the potatoes are cooked turn off or switch off the heat, then ask a grown-up to carry the pan of very hot vegetables to the sink.

**7** Watch how they strain the vegetables through a sieve or colander – also see page 77.

**8** Tip the potatoes back into the saucepan and break up with a fork, then continue beating with the fork or with a potato masher until they are quite soft.

**9** Add half the margarine, save the rest, and gradually beat in the milk. Use a wooden spoon for this.

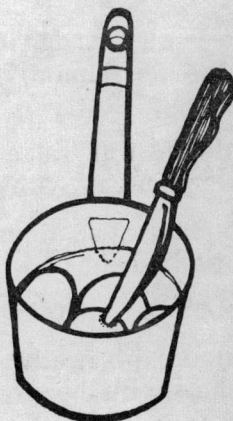

**10** Add the pepper, then taste and add a little more salt if necessary. Keep the potatoes in the pan while you prepare the filling.

**11** Set you oven to moderate, 375°F, 190°C or gas mark 5.

**12** Open the can of salmon, or ask a grown-up to do this for you.

**13** Tip the salmon into a basin and take out the skin and the bones as you do not use these.

**14** Halve the lemon and squeeze the juice from one half. Cut the other half into 2 or 3 slices; this is quite an awkward job, so you may prefer to ask a grown-up to help. These slices are for garnish.

**15** Mix the lemon juice with the salmon.

**16** Break the first egg into a cup, then tip it into the salmon; repeat with the second egg.

**17** Add the milk, salt and pepper and mix together well with a fork.

**18** Spoon the fish mixture into the oven-proof dish.

**19** Spoon the potato mixture on top.

**20** Smooth this neatly with the knife, then mark with the prongs of a fork.

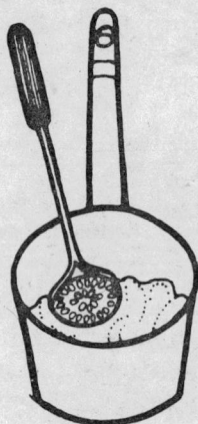

**21** Dot the rest of the margarine over the top in very tiny pieces.

**22** Bake in the centre of a moderate oven for 30 minutes.

**23** Lift out and put a sprig of parsley and the lemon slices on top.

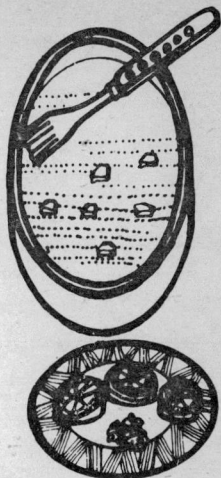

## To make a change

**Tuna pie.** Use canned tuna fish instead of salmon.

**Fish pie.** Simmer 450g (1 lb) white fish or smoked haddock fillet in water until tender, this takes about 10 minutes. Add a little salt when cooking white fish – cod, fresh haddock, etc. – but no salt when cooking smoked haddock. Make sure the water does not boil too quickly.

Strain the fish in the same way as vegetables, page 82, put it into a basin and take away any skin.

You then make the recipe in exactly the same way as salmon pie, stage 14–17, page 71.

**Vegetable pie.** Peel about 450 g (1 lb) mixed root vegetables (carrots, turnip, part of a swede or a small parsnip). Cut the vegetables into 1.5–2.5 cm (½–1 inch) dice, or ask a grown-up to do this awkward job for you. Cook and strain the vegetables in boiling salted water as described when cooking potatoes as stages 4–7, but allow only 10–15 minutes. Continue as stages 16–17 using the vegetables instead of the salmon.

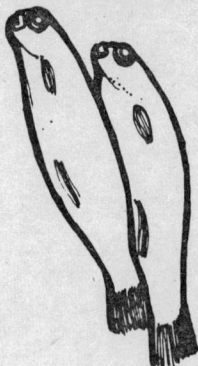

# Bacon and spaghetti hotch potch

This is a splendid dish for supper. It takes only a few minutes to cook and you cook everything in one big frying pan or saucepan.

**You will need:**

| | |
|---|---|
| *bacon* | 4 rashers |
| *margarine* | small knob |
| *spaghetti in tomato sauce* | 1 medium can |
| *eggs* | 4 |
| *milk* | 4 tablespoons |
| *salt* | pinch |

*These ingredients will make 4 servings*

**You will use:**
plates for ingredients, kitchen scissors or a sharp knife and chopping board, large frying pan, small knife, can opener, wooden spoon, cup, basin, tablespoon, fork, serving plates.

**For success:**
Do not over-cook at stage 10 otherwise the mixture will be dry.

**1** Cut off the bacon rinds and cut the bacon into neat strips with the kitchen scissors or a sharp knife on the chopping board.

**2** Put the bacon rinds and the bacon pieces into the frying pan, and place this on the burner or hotplate.

**3** Light the gas burner or switch on the electric hotplate.

**4** Cook the bacon and the bacon rinds for 2 minutes, then put a piece of margarine from the packet – about the size of a walnut – into the frying pan.

**5** Move the frying pan away from the heat and lift out the bacon rinds – you will not eat these, but they have given extra fat.

**6** Open the can of spaghetti or ask a grown-up to do this.

**7** Tip the spaghetti into the pan and put it back over the heat; stir well with a wooden spoon.

**8** Break the first egg into the cup, then tip it into the basin; continue like this with the other eggs.

**9** Add the milk and salt; beat with a fork.

**10** Pour the egg mixture into the pan, *lower* the heat and stir carefully for 2–3 minutes only, then serve at once.

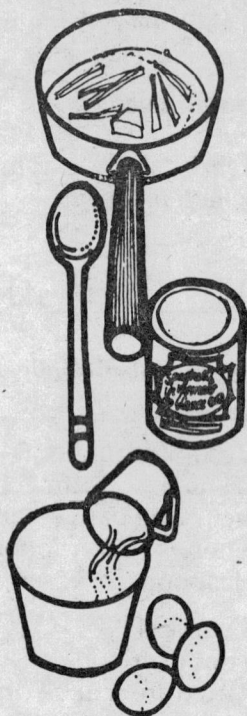

# Cheese and apple salad

This is a pretty salad for a party supper dish.

**You will need:**

| | |
|---|---|
| *lettuce* | 1 |
| *mayonnaise or* | |
| *salad dressing* | 4 tablespoons |
| *milk* | 1 tablespoon |
| *vinegar* | 1 teaspoon |
| *red-skinned dessert* | |
| *apples* | 2 |
| *orange* | 1 |
| *Cheddar cheese* | about 225 grammes (8 oz) |

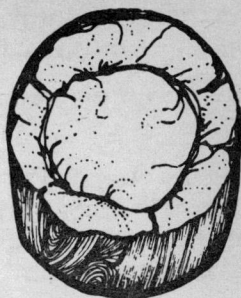

*These ingredients will make 4–5 servings.*

**You will use:**
plates for ingredients, salad shaker or cloth, tablespoon, teaspoon, mixing bowl, chopping board, sharp knife, serving dish.

**For success:**
Put the apple into the mayonnaise mixture as soon as it is cut. This stops it turning a brown colour.

**1** Wash the lettuce in cold water. Shake dry in a salad shaker or pat *gently* in a cloth.

**2** Put the mayonnaise or salad dressing, milk and vinegar into the mixing bowl.

**3** Wash and dry, but do not peel, the apples. Put them on to the chopping board; halve, then quarter, and cut away the cores.

**4** Cut the apples into neat small pieces, or ask a grown-up to do this for you.

**5** Tip into the mayonnaise mixture and stir.

**6** Peel the orange. Put the segments of fruit on to the chopping board or on to a plate and cut neatly, then add to the apple mixture, discard the orange pips.

**7** Put the cheese on to the chopping board, cut it into neat pieces and add these to the apple mixture.

**8** Lay the lettuce on the serving dish and spoon the cheese and apple mixture in the centre.

## Did you know?

There are several ways to chop parsley. Always wash *and* dry the parsley first and remove all the stalks.

**1** Put the sprigs on to a chopping board and chop in a clockwise direction. As you will see from the picture the finger tips of your left hand support one end of the knife (the non-cutting edge).

**2** Use kitchen scissors. This is a good way as the parsley juice is not wasted.

**3** Use one of the special choppers or a food processor.

# Did you know?

The way to tell if fat is hot enough for frying is to melt the fat and put a tiny cube of bread into the pan; if it turns golden brown *in about 1 minute* you can cook the food. If it burns or browns more quickly allow the fat to cool slightly and test again.

Always pull the frying pan away from the heat as you test.

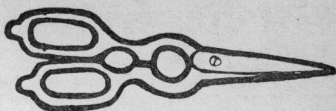

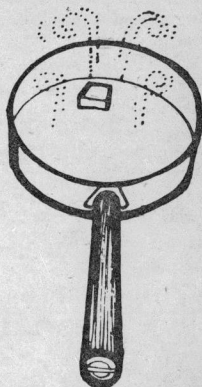

# Did you know?

There are two ways of straining vegetables. Both mean handling hot saucepans filled with hot food and liquid, so a grown-up should do them generally.

1 Take the pan to the sink and tilt the lid so the liquid can run into the sink, or into a large basin in the sink. This is very difficult.

2 Put a colander or big sieve over a large basin in the sink or put these into the sink. Tip the vegetables *carefully* into the sieve or colander. *Mind the steam*.

# Dishes from other countries

When you visit other countries you have the opportunity to try new foods and interesting dishes. Some of these dishes can be made when you get home.

Hamburgers are a favourite dish in America. You will find a recipe on pages 62 and 63 in **The Piccolo Cookbook** and another recipe in this book on pages 62–5.

Croque monsieur is the name given to a French fried sandwich filled with cheese and ham. The recipe follows on the next page together with ideas for varying this, including an Italian version of the recipe.

One of the famous French salads is called salad niçoise (it originated from Nice in the south of France). The recipe starts on page 90.

Italians love pizzas and all forms of pasta (the name given to food made from wheat; this includes spaghetti, macaroni, and other interesting shapes).

Spaghetti bolognese is one of the more popular pasta dishes. You will find the recipe on pages 85–9. A quick and easy recipe for making a pizza is on pages 82–84. On page 112 a dish based on Chinese foods begins.

# Croque monsieur

This is a well-known French recipe. It is very easy and quick to make. There is another recipe for fried sandwiches called cheese dreams in **The Piccolo Cookbook** on pages 54–5.

**You will need:**

| | |
|---|---|
| *bread* | 4 large slices |
| *butter or margarine* | 25 grammes (1 oz) |
| *Gruyère, Cheddar or processed cheese* | 2 slices |
| *cooked ham* | 2 slices |

for coating:

| | |
|---|---|
| *egg* | 1 |
| *milk* | 2 tablespoons |

for frying:

| | |
|---|---|
| *fat or butter* | 50 grammes (2 oz) |

*These ingredients will make 4 small or 2 large servings.*

**You will use:**
plates for ingredients, sharp knife, bread board, flat-bladed knife, large shallow dish, tablespoon, fork, frying pan, fish slice, serving plate.

**For success:**
Do not over-cook the sandwiches otherwise the cheese will be tough.

**1** Cut four slices of bread, or take four slices of ready cut bread.

**2** Spread the bread with butter or margarine.

**3** Cover 2 slices of bread with layers of cheese and ham; top with the other slices of bread. Cut each sandwich into half.

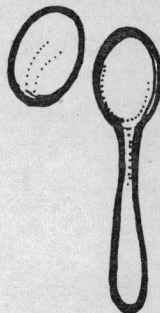

**4** Break the egg on to the shallow dish, add the milk and beat with the fork.

**5** Carry the dish near the cooker so you do not have egg 'drips' on the floor.

**6** Dip the sandwiches into the egg mixture for ½ minute only; turn them over and dip the second side in the egg mixture.

**7** Put the fat or butter into the frying pan.

**8** Light the gas burner or switch on the electric hotplate.

**9** Heat the fat or butter until it has just melted – do not get it too hot; then lower the heat.

**10** Lift the first sandwich off the dish and put it carefully into the fat or butter. Do this with the other sandwiches.

**11** Cook the sandwiches for nearly 1½ minutes on the bottom side, turn over with the fish slice and cook for the same time on the second side.

**12** Lift out on to the warmed serving plate and serve at once. These are very good with a salad or raw tomatoes.

## To make a change

**Fried ham and chutney sandwiches.**
Spread half the slices of buttered bread
with chutney, then top with the ham
and remaining slices of buttered bread.
Do not use cheese. Halve the
sandwiches and then continue as
stages 4–12.

**Fried fish and cheese sandwiches.**
Spread half the slices of buttered bread
with well-drained and flaked canned
tuna or salmon. Top with cottage or
cream cheese and the remaining slices
of buttered bread. Halve the
sandwiches, then continue as stages 4–
12.

**Formaggio in carrozza.** This means
'cheese in a carriage'. Prepare the
cheese and ham sandwiches as stages
1–5 on page 79–80. In addition to the
egg mixture have a second plate or dish
or sheet of greaseproof paper, spread
with 50 grammes (2oz) fine soft
breadcrumbs. Dip the sandwiches in
the egg mixture as stage 6, then into the
breadcrumbs. Make sure both sides of
the sandwiches are coated. Heat the fat
or butter in a large frying pan as stages
7, 8 and 9. Fry the sandwiches as stages
10–12. These sandwiches are nicer if
drained on a sheet of kitchen paper
after frying.

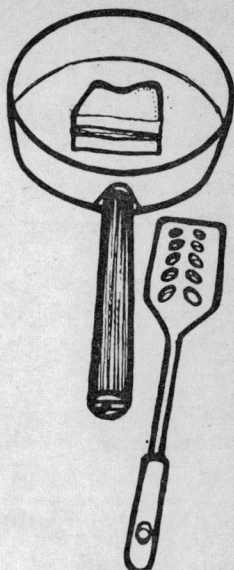

# Speedy pizzas

Pizza pie is a dish you will find when you visit Italy; this is a very quick version of that well-known savoury.

**You will need:**

| | |
|---|---|
| *tomatoes* | 4 large |
| *water* | 2 tablespoons |
| *onion* | 1 small |
| *salt* | pinch |
| *pepper* | shake |
| *round rolls* | 4 large |
| *anchovy fillets* | 1 can |
| *Cheddar cheese* | about 50 grammes (2 oz) |

*little butter or margarine (optional)*

*These ingredients will make 4 large or 8 small servings.*

**You will use:**
plates for ingredients, chopping board, sharp knife, saucepan, tablespoon, grater, wooden spoon, flat knife, fish slice, serving dish.

**For success:**
Have the grill very hot before heating the pizzas at stage 10.

**1** Cut the tomatoes into slices, then put into a saucepan with the water.

**2** Peel the onion and rub against the coarse side of the grater; let the onion drop into the saucepan.

**3** Light the gas burner or switch on the electric hotplate.

**4** Cook the tomato mixture for about 5 minutes until it becomes quite thick. Stir with the wooden spoon as the mixture cooks, so that it does not burn.

**5** Take the pan off the heat and add the salt and pepper to the tomato mixture.

**6** Split the rolls and toast them under the grill; you can spread them with butter or margarine if you like.

**7** Spread the tomato mixture over the halved rolls and stand them in the grill pan.

**8** Open the can of anchovy fillets or ask a grown-up to do this for you. Lift out the anchovy fillets and arrange them on top of the tomato mixture in a neat design.

**9** Grate the cheese and sprinkle it over the top of the tomato and anchovy mixture.

**10** Put under the hot grill and heat for about 2 minutes, until the cheese has melted, then lift on to a serving dish and serve at once.

*Note!* You could cook the tomato mixture earlier in the day, so it is quite ready before you make the pizzas.

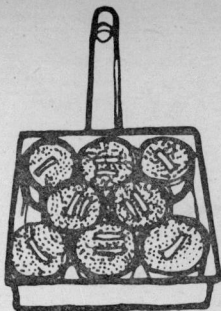

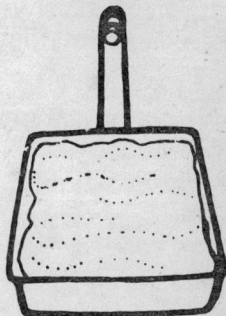

## To make a change

Use canned sardines in place of
anchovy fillets.

Cut cooked ham or salami into neat
strips and use instead of anchovy
fillets.

**Bacon pizza.** Omit the anchovy fillets
and use 2–3 bacon rashers. Remove the
bacon rinds and cut the bacon into
narrow strips. Arrange the bacon on
top of the grated cheese and continue
as stage 10 above.

Instead of using fresh tomatoes use a
medium size can of tomatoes. Open the
can or ask an adult to do this for you.

Put the tomatoes with 3 tablespoons
liquid from the can into the saucepan
and continue as stages 2–5.

# Spaghetti bolognese

This is the name given to spaghetti and a meat sauce. The sauce can be served with crisp toast or mixed vegetables instead of spaghetti. If any is left over, serve it as a filling for pancakes, pages 34–7 tell you how to make these.

The recipe for the sauce is similar to the one the Italians would use, but some ingredients are marked 'optional'. This is because they can be omitted if you do not have them in the kitchen.

## You will need:

for the sauce:

| | |
|---|---|
| medium onion | 1 |
| garlic clove, optional | 1 |
| medium carrot, optional | 1 |
| medium tomatoes | 4 |
| mushrooms | 50–100 grammes (2–4 oz) |
| parsley | medium sprig |
| olive oil or corn oil or any good frying oil | 2 tablespoons |
| raw minced beef | 225–350 grammes (8–12 oz) |
| hot water | 284 ml (½ pint) |
| beef stock cube | ½ |
| tomato purée (from a tube or can) | 1 tablespoon |
| salt | pinch |
| pepper | shake |
| water | 2. 4 litres (4 pints) |
| salt | 1 level teaspoon |
| spaghetti | 225 g (8 oz) |

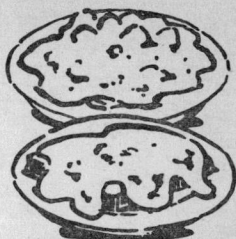

| Parmesan or Cheddar cheese | 40–50 grammes (1½–2 oz) |

*These ingredients will make 4 servings for a substantial snack.*

**You will use:**
plates for ingredients, chopping board, sharp knife, 2 tablespoons, grater, 1 medium saucepan, 1 very large saucepan, wooden spoon, measure, teaspoon, colander, serving dish.

**For success:**
Make quite sure the sauce has plenty of flavour. Do not over-cook the spaghetti, keep the water boiling steadily as it cooks.

**1** Peel the onion and chop it finely or ask a grown-up to do this for you.

**2** Take a clove from the head of garlic; skin this and chop it or ask a grown-up to do the rather difficult job. Wash your hands after handling garlic.

**3** Peel the carrot and rub this against the coarse side of a grater.

**4** Slice the tomatoes, they can be skinned, see under the *Note!* at the end of the method.

**5** Cut a very thin slice from the bottom of the stalk of each mushroom.

**6** Wipe the mushrooms with a clean damp cloth or moist kitchen paper or wash them in cold water and dry them well. There is no need to skin them.

**7** Cut the mushrooms into slices.

**8** Chop the parsley in one of the ways given in the directions on page 76. You need about 1 tablespoon when chopped.

**9** Measure out the oil and put this into the medium-sized saucepan.

**10** Light the gas burner or switch on the electric hotplate; heat the oil for 1 minute, do not allow it to become too hot.

**11** Add the onion, garlic and carrot and turn the vegetables in the oil with the wooden spoon.

**12** Add the mushrooms, tomatoes and meat to the onion and garlic and stir over a low heat for 2–3 minutes. Take the pan off the heat while you follow stages 13–15.

**13** Pour 284 ml (½ pint) of hot water into the measure, blend the stock cube with this and add this liquid to the other ingredients in the saucepan.

**14** Measure out the tomato purée from the tube (some people buy it in a can), add to the meat mixture.

**15** Add half the parsley to the other ingredients in the saucepan, together with a little salt and pepper.

**16** Return the pan to the heat and stir several times until the mixture reaches simmering point.

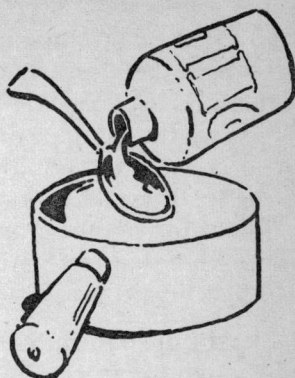

**17** Put a lid on the saucepan and turn the heat very low, the sauce takes 45 minutes to cook. You will need to remove the lid once or twice and stir the sauce. This should be fairly thick. If it is too thin at the end of the cooking time remove the lid and cook more quickly for about 5 minutes so the excess liquid evaporates.

**18** About 20 minutes before the sauce is cooked pour the 2.4 litres (4 pints) of water into the large saucepan.

**19** Add the teaspoon of salt and bring the water to boiling point.

**20** Ask a grown-up to help you add the spaghetti, for this is quite difficult. Hold the ends in one hand and lower these into the boiling salted water.

**21** As soon as the ends soften turn the spaghetti so all the strands are in the water. Do not cover the saucepan.

**22** Cook as the timing on the packet, but use the 2 tablespoons and lift the spaghetti once at least during the cooking period to separate the strands.

**23** While the spaghetti and sauce cook grate the cheese, although Parmesan cheese is often sold ready-grated in little drums. Lift out one strand of spaghetti, cool slightly and taste it when you *think* it will be cooked. The spaghetti should be soft, but not over-soft.

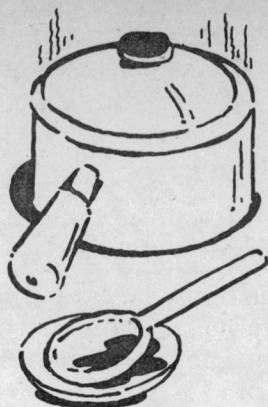

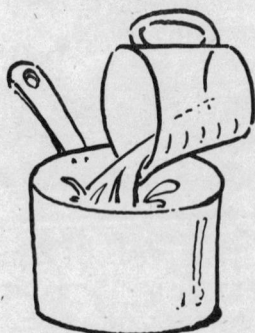

**24** Taste the sauce, add a little more salt and pepper if necessary.

**25** Strain the spaghetti through a colander. Put on to the heated serving dish.

**26** Spoon the sauce over the spaghetti.

**27** Top with the remaining parsley.

**28** Serve with the grated cheese.

*Note!* To skin tomatoes, heat a little water in a saucepan, lower the first tomato into this with a tablespoon. Leave in the water for about ½ minute, remove and put into cold water. You then can pull away the skin with your fingers. Continue like this.

# Salad niçoise

This is the kind of salad you can have for a light snack or a main meal. The vegetables given are the usual ones for this well-known salad, but you could substitute others if you wish. Prepare the lettuce and the eggs ahead so the lettuce dries and the eggs have time to cool, see pages 42, stages 4–6 for details of boiling eggs. Anchovy fillets and black olives are very popular in France and part of the classic recipe. If you leave these out you could call the dish a 'summer salad', for the vegetables used are plentiful in summer.

## You will need:

| | |
|---|---|
| small lettuce | 1 |
| hard-boiled eggs | 2 |
| cooked new potatoes | 225 grammes (8 oz) |
| cooked French or runner beans | 225 grammes (8 oz) |
| medium cucumber | about ¼ |
| medium tomatoes | 3–4 |
| small green pepper | 1 |
| tuna fish | 1 medium can |
| anchovy fillets | 1 small can |
| black olives | about 8 |

for the dressing:

| | |
|---|---|
| olive oil or corn oil or good salad oil or see stages 8 and 11 | 2 tablespoons |
| vinegar | 1 tablespoon |
| salt | pinch |
| pepper | shake |
| sugar | pinch |

*These ingredients will make 4–5 servings.*

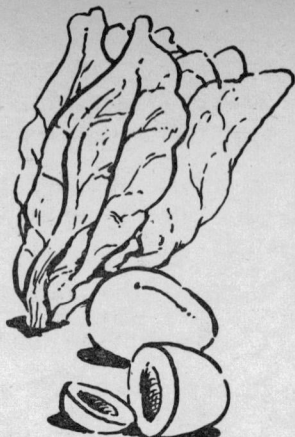

**You will use:**

plates for ingredients, saucepan, salad shaker or a cloth or kitchen paper, chopping board, small sharp knife, can opener, salad bowl, basin or screw topped jar, teaspoon.

**For success:**

Make sure the ingredients are neatly sliced and the salad looks attractive.

**1** Wash the lettuce, shake it dry in a salad shaker or pat it gently in a clean cloth or kitchen paper.

**2** Shell and slice the eggs, then slice the potatoes, beans, cucumber and tomatoes.

**3** Wipe the green pepper, cut a slice from the stalk end.

**4** Put your fingers inside the pepper and pull out the centre (called the core) and all the seeds. These taste very hot so it is important to get rid of them; you can rinse the pepper under the cold tap to be sure of this.

**5** Cut all the flesh of the pepper into neat strips, including the slice removed, do not use the stalk.

**6** Put the lettuce into the salad bowl and the eggs and all the vegetables.

**7** Open the cans of tuna and anchovies or ask a grown-up to do this; anchovy cans are different from most cans in shape and the way they are opened.

**8** Pour away any oil from the fish; in this recipe you could use this fish-flavoured oil as part of the dressing so pour it into the basin or jar.

**9**  Arrange the tuna fish and anchovy fillets on top of the salad; you can lift the anchovy fillets from the can with the tip of the knife.

**10**  Remove the olives from the jar with a teaspoon, place over the fish.

**11**  The salad is then ready, except for the dressing. Pour the oil into the basin or jar; if you have used some fish oil add just enough extra oil to make 2 tablespoons.

**12**  Add the vinegar, salt, pepper and sugar and mix well with a wooden spoon or fasten the lid of the jar and shake the ingredients together.

**13**  Pour this dressing over the salad just before it is served.

# Hot milk drinks

In **The Piccolo Cookbook** you had recipes for coffee, tea and some milky drinks, but I thought you would like some more ideas. The following recipes are all made with hot milk and are served in a large mug, cup or tumbler (make sure the tumbler is strong enough to hold hot milk). If you are trying to lose weight, choose skimmed milk, and reduce the amount of sugar and sweets used.

**Banana whip.** Mash a small banana with 1 tablespoon sugar. Divide it between 2 mugs, cups or tumblers. Add hot milk to these.

**Honey and cinnamon milk.** Put ½–1 tablespoon honey into each container. Add the hot milk and sprinkle ground cinnamon over the top.

**Marshmallow surprise.** Heat the milk, pour it into the container. Float marshmallows on top (choose the pink ones if possible, they look prettier). Serve with a spoon so that you can eat the half-melted marshmallows.

**Peppermint milk.** Heat the milk, pour it into the container. Float 2–3 plain or chocolate-coated peppermint creams in the milk and stir gently until they dissolve.

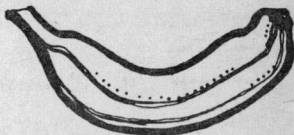

# Cold milk drinks

These cold milk drinks look nicer in a glass tumbler than in a cup or mug. If you make the edge of the tumbler damp by dipping it in cold water then turn it upside down over a plate with a little caster sugar, you have a very pretty edge. Use skimmed rather than full-cream milk to lower the calories.

**Mocha surprise.** Put a spoonful of chocolate ice-cream into the tumbler. Half fill with fairly weak coffee, top with really cold milk.

**Ginger fizz.** Half fill the tumbler with really cold milk, then top up with ginger beer or ginger ale.

**Peppermint ice-cream soda.** Half fill the tumbler with really cold milk. Add enough soda water to make the drink come three-quarters of the way up the tumbler. Float 2–3 teaspoons ice-cream and 2–3 plain or chocolate-coated peppermint creams on top. Serve with a teaspoon.

**Banana ice-cream soda.** Half fill the tumbler with really cold milk. Add enough soda water to make the drink come three-quarters of the way up the tumbler. Add a tablespoon of strawberry ice-cream and a few banana slices.

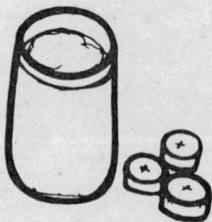

# Make a good dinner

If you can cook a complete dinner it will be a lovely surprise and treat for the family, and I am sure you can do it well if you plan everything carefully.

Never try to cook a whole dinner yourself without asking permission from your parents, for food (particularly meat or chicken) is expensive and they may prefer to help you. If they say 'yes' then you can feel very proud of doing such an important job.

## Meal in a parcel

This meal 'looks after itself' as you wrap all the food in squares of aluminium foil. Do not waste this after use, wash it carefully and allow it to dry.

**You will need:**

| | |
|---|---|
| *lamb chops* | 4 lean |
| *tomatoes* | 4 large |
| *potatoes* | 4 large |
| *salt* | pinch |
| *pepper* | shake |
| *frozen beans* | 1 packet (for 4) |
| *margarine* | 15 grammes (½ oz) |

*These ingredients will make 4 servings.*

**You will use:**
plates for ingredients, aluminium foil,
kitchen scissors, sharp knife, chopping
board, potato peeler or vegetable knife,
bowl, baking or meat tin, serving dish.

**For success:**
Wrap the foil parcels lightly.

1  Look at the lamb chops and if they
seem to have a lot of fat cut this away,
then decide on the size of the
aluminium squares – you need 4 for the
chops, tomatoes and potatoes and 1
large one for the beans. The foil must be
sufficiently large to make a complete
covering for the food.

2  Put the 4 lamb chops in the middle of
the 4 good-sized squares of foil.

3  Cut each tomato in 3–4 thick slices
and put these on top of the chops.

4  Peel the potatoes and cut each one
into 6–7 thin slices, or ask a grown-up
to do this for you; keep the potatoes in a
bowl of water as you peel them so they
do not discolour, rinse well in cold
water.

5  Put the potato slices over the
tomatoes and add the salt and pepper;
be sparing with this as there is no water
with the food. Wrap up these four
parcels carefully.

6  Tip the frozen beans on to the large
piece of foil, add the margarine, salt
and pepper, and wrap up carefully.

7  Place the 5 foil parcels on to the
baking or meat tin.

**8** You can set the oven before you begin this recipe, but this is the kind of meal you can put into an automatic oven and leave for some time; ask a grown-up to tell you about this kind of oven. Set your oven to moderate, 375°F, 190°C, gas mark 5.

**9** Put the parcels into the centre of the moderate oven.

**10** Leave for 55 minutes, then lift out carefully.

**11** Ask a grown-up to open the parcels for you or use oven gloves, for a lot of steam comes out.

**12** Lift the food on to a hot dish.

**13** You may need to strain the beans, see page 77. Serve at once.

# A roast dinner

A roast meal, such as you might eat for a Sunday lunch, sounds complicated but in fact it is not difficult to cook. It does mean taking great care not to hurt yourself on hot tins, and it does mean 'dishing up' in the right order, so that none of the food becomes cold before it is served. Page 106 tells you about this.

As meat for roasting is expensive, you will probably need a grown-up's agreement before tackling the following menu:

Roast lamb
Mint sauce
Roast potatoes
Cauliflower or other green vegetable
Fruit trifle (see page 163)
or fruit salad and cream (see page 164)

**You will need:**
ingredients for fruit trifle (page 163) or
fruit salad (page 164)

| | |
|---|---|
| *potatoes* | 675 grammes (1½ lb) |
| *lamb* | ½ leg or ½ shoulder |
| *fat (optional)* | 50 grammes (2 oz) |

for the sauce:
| | |
|---|---|
| *mint* | small bunch |
| *sugar* | 1–2 tablespoons |
| *vinegar* | 2 tablespoons |

| | |
|---|---|
| *cauliflower* | 1 |
| *salt* | very good pinch |

for the gravy:
| | |
|---|---|
| *flour* | 1 tablespoon |
| *gravy browning* | ½ tablespoon |
| *water** | 142 ml (¼ pint) |
| *vegetable water** | 142 ml (¼ pint) |
| *fat from cooking the meat* | 1 tablespoon |

*These ingredients will make 4 servings.*
There will probably be some cooked
meat left. This can be served cold.

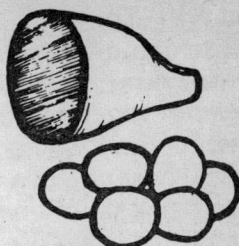

* You may prefer to use stock made by
simmering meat bones in water.

## You will use:

plates for ingredients, utensils for trifle or fruit salad, pages 163 or 164, potato peeler or vegetable knife, bowl, roasting tin, kitchen paper, sharp knife, chopping board (or kitchen scissors), 2 sauce boats, 2 tablespoons, clean teacloth (or use kitchen paper), meat dish, serving dish for cauliflower, serving plates, colander, 1 fairly large saucepan with lid, 1 smaller saucepan, teaspoon, wooden spoon, basin, fish slice.

## For success:

Make out your timetable and work carefully and steadily through this; do not try and do too many things at one time.

1 Make the trifle or fruit salad before you prepare the meat and potatoes, so that it is quite ready. You could make the trifle the day beforehand, but the fruit salad is nicer if prepared only a few hours before it is served.

2 Put the trifle or fruit salad into a cool place.

3 Peel the potatoes and keep in a bowl of cold water so they do not become dark in colour – *halve large potatoes*.

4 Weigh the meat, or look at the ticket from the butcher or supermarket; this is important, for you work out the cooking time according to the weight of the meat. When cooking lamb you

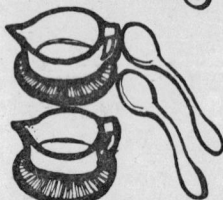

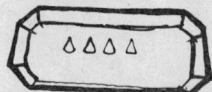

allow 20 minutes for each 450 grammes (1 lb) plus an extra 20 minutes, if the meat is home produced, but see page 107.

A joint weighing 1.35kg. (3lb) would take:

| | |
|---|---|
| 3 x 20 minutes | = 1 hour |
| plus extra 20 minutes | = 20 minutes |
| | |
| Total cooking time | = 1 hour 20 minutes |

**5** Put the meat into the roasting tin, and it is a good idea to choose a tin sufficiently large to cook the potatoes in it as well as the meat.

**6** Add the fat to the meat in the tin; if you are roasting lamb without roasting potatoes you will not need this fat.

**7** Now look at the clock. You do not want to heat the oven, or put the meat into the oven too soon for if you do it will be over-cooked.

**8** If you are putting the meat into *a cold oven*, then lighting the gas or switching on the electric oven, add an extra 10 minutes to your total cooking time; the meat starts to cook in the heating-up period.

If you are putting the meat into *a heated oven*, then light the gas or switch on the electric oven and wait 15 minutes before putting in the meat.

**9** Let us imagine you want the meat at 1 p.m. and that the joint takes 1 hour 20 minutes to cook and that you are putting the meat into a cold oven. This is the timetable to follow:

**10** *11.25 a.m.:* put the meat in its tin (with the fat) into the oven.

In most gas ovens you put it towards the top of the oven.

In many electric ovens too you can put it near the top of the oven, but in some other electric cookers it is better to put the meat in its tin at the bottom of the oven – *check with your mother or with the card or book that goes with your cooker. If the electric oven is fan assisted the position does not matter.*

**11** Set your oven to moderately hot: usually 400°F, 200°C or gas mark 6. Cookers vary slightly so *just check* with the card or book that goes with your cooker.

**12** You can now prepare the mint sauce. Wash the mint in cold water and take the leaves from the stalks. Pat these dry on kitchen paper. Chop the mint with a sharp knife (this is quite difficult) on the chopping board, or use kitchen scissors. Page 76 tells you how to chop parsley, and mint is chopped in the same way.

**13** Put the mint into the sauce boat, add the sugar and vinegar, and stir well.

*Note!* If you don't know anyone who grows mint, you can sometimes find it in supermarkets or greengrocers. Otherwise, buy a jar of mint concentrate and follow the directions on it.

**14** *11.50 a.m.:* lift the potatoes out of the bowl of cold water and dry them very well on kitchen paper or a clean teacloth.

**15** *11.55 a.m.: at this stage you must be very careful, or you must ask a grown-up to help you.* Open the oven door and take the meat tin out of the oven. You must have *strong oven gloves* and you must make sure *no one is near enough to distract you* or is playing in the kitchen. Put the very hot tin down – *make sure you do not burn any surface* – some modern laminated working surfaces can be harmed with very hot tins, so it is a good idea to put a cork mat under the tin. *Make sure the tin cannot be tipped over.* Close the oven door.

**16** Put the potatoes into the hot fat.

**17** Now take the 2 tablespoons and turn the potatoes round in the hot fat, so that they look greasy on all sides.

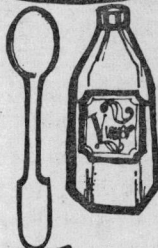

**18** Open the oven door again and put the tin back into the oven.

**19** There is no need to touch the tin or oven again until it is time to dish up.

**20** *12.05 p.m.:* prepare the cauliflower. You can cook it whole, but you save more of the vitamin C (see page 31) if you divide the flower part into neat sprigs. Use some of the inner green stalks, but not the very outside stalks. Wash the cauliflower in cold water, then lift it into a colander and allow it to drain.

**21** *12.15 p.m.:* put the serving dishes and the plates to warm.

**22** *12.20 p.m.:* fill the larger saucepan with water to a height of about 8 cm (3 inches) and add a very good pinch of salt (or use ¼ teaspoon).

**23** Take this to the cooker, and light the gas burner or switch on the electric hotplate.

**24** *12.25 p.m.:* blend the flour and gravy browning with 142ml (¼ pint) of water in a basin.

**25** Tip into the smaller saucepan.

**26** *12.30 p.m.:* carry the cauliflower in the colander to the cooker. If you stand the colander on a plate you will have no 'drips' of cold water.

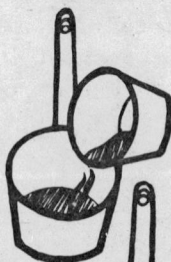

**27** Put the cauliflower into the boiling water and cover the saucepan with a lid.

**28** *12.45 p.m.:* turn off the burner or hotplate. Take the cauliflower pan to the sink and strain this or ask a grown-up to do this (see page 82). Save 142 ml or ¼ pint of the liquid. Put the cauliflower into a serving dish *and keep it warm.*

**29** Pour the 142ml (¼ pint) of cauliflower water into the flour and gravy browning saucepan (see stages 24 and 25).

**30** Light the gas burner or switch on the electric hotplate again and stir the gravy with the wooden spoon until it thickens; turn the heat very low to keep it hot.

**31** *12.58 p.m.:* take the meat tin out of the oven. *Remember all the points mentioned in stage 15.*

**32** Lift the meat and potatoes on to the hot meat dish – a fish slice is good for this.

**33** Turn off the burner or hotplate and carry the gravy saucepan *very carefully* over to the meat tin. Stir in 1 tablespoon of the fat from the tin. If the gravy is really hot you will not need to cook it again.

**34** Pour the gravy into the sauce boat and the meal is ready.

As you will see you have to be rather quick between stages 26 and 34.

You may find it easier to dish up the meat and potatoes a little earlier and keep them hot, in which case start the cooking 5 minutes earlier.

Grown-ups will probably prefer to dish up the cauliflower at the last minute – this is the best way to cook vegetables, so they are not being kept warm for too long – but you will need practice to do everything 'all at once' and it is better to work steadily when you are learning to cook.

## Cooking frozen meat

Much of the meat we buy today has been frozen. Sometimes people buy fresh meat and freeze it in their own freezer, at other times they buy ready-frozen meat from the freezer shop or supermarket.

Chops and steaks and chicken joints can be cooked without defrosting them. Larger joints are better defrosted (thawed out) before cooking and whole chickens or other poultry *must be completely defrosted* before cooking.

As well as frozen meat we can buy imported meat from other countries. In order to keep it in perfect condition the meat must be well-chilled during transport.

Defrosted frozen and chilled joints are better cooked more slowly than the timing given on page 101, stage 4, so if you are cooking imported lamb allow the following temperature and cooking times.

Set the oven to very moderate to moderate 325–350°F, 160–180°C or gas mark 3–4. The difference in setting is because ovens vary, so consult a grown-up about the better temperature to use.

A joint weighing 1.35 kg (3 lb) would take:

3 x 35 minutes = 105 minutes (1 hour 25 minutes)
plus extra 35 minutes = 35 minutes

Total cooking time = 140 minutes (2 hours 20 minutes)

# Hunter's chicken casserole

This is a very good way of cooking chicken; you do not need to make a gravy and the tomatoes and vegetables in the recipe take the place of a green vegetable. Serve with jacket potatoes to make a good meal.

## You will need:

| | |
|---|---|
| *frying chicken* | 4 portions |
| *potatoes* | 4 medium |
| *margarine* | 50 grammes (2 oz) |
| *tomatoes* | 1 medium can |
| *onion* | 1 large |
| *carrot* | 1 large |
| *salt* | good pinch |
| *pepper* | good shake |

to garnish:
*parsley*          small sprig

*These ingredients will make 4 servings.*

## You will use:

plates for ingredients, kitchen paper, scrubbing brush, baking tray, fork, flat-bladed knife, oven-proof casserole with a lid, 2 tablespoons, can opener, basin, sharp knife, grater, teacloth, vegetable dish for potatoes.

## For success:

Let the chicken brown at stage 10 before you add the tomato mixture. Do not over-cook chicken; it makes it very dry.

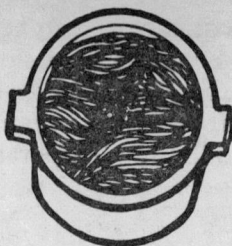

**1** If you are using portions of frozen chicken allow these to thaw (defrost) at room temperature before cooking. This must be done thoroughly and will take 8–12 hours. If using joints of fresh chicken wash them in cold water, then dry them on kitchen paper. Dry frozen chicken in the same way when it has defrosted.

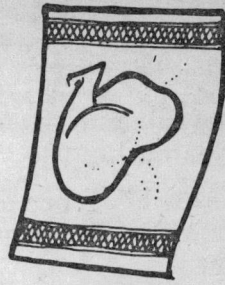

**2** Set your oven to very moderate, 325°F, 160°C or gas mark 3.

**3** Scrub and dry the potatoes, put them on the baking tray (this makes it easier to take them out of the oven), and prick them with a fork so that they do not burst their skins.

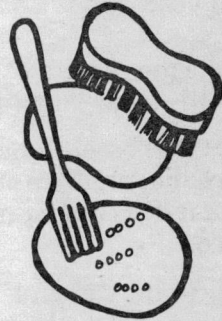

**4** Put the potatoes towards the top of the oven.

**5** Put the margarine into the casserole, place it in the centre of the oven and leave it for 5 minutes so that the margarine melts.

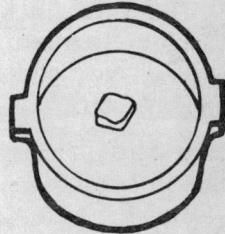

**6** Remove the casserole from the oven; read page 103 stage 15, about taking hot tins or dishes from a hot oven.

**7** Put the casserole on to the working surface, taking care it does not harm this; it is always a good idea to put a pan stand or cork mat under hot dishes.

**8** Add the pieces of chicken and turn them in the melted margarine with the 2 tablespoons.

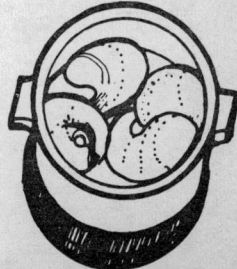

**9** Put the casserole back into the oven; do not cover it for you want the chicken to brown slightly.

**10** Leave the chicken for 15 minutes without touching it.

**11** Meanwhile, open the can of tomatoes, or ask a grown-up to do this for you.

**12** Tip the tomatoes into a basin, and chop them with a knife and fork.

**13** Grate the peeled onion and carrot into the tomatoes. Add the salt and pepper.

**14** Take the casserole with the chicken out of the oven – do this very carefully.

**15** Put the casserole on to the working surface. Be careful to stand it on a mat, so that it does not harm the working surface.

**16** Allow the casserole to stand for about 5 minutes, then pour the tomato mixture over the chicken. If you pour the cold tomato mixture over the very hot chicken you could crack an oven-proof glass dish.

**17** Put the lid on the casserole, replace it in the centre of the oven and leave for 40 minutes.

**18** Remove the casserole from the oven.

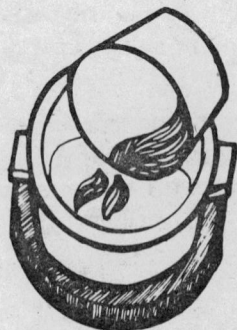

**19**  Most casseroles can be used for serving dishes, so take off the lid – *do this very carefully for there will be a lot of steam coming from the dish* – and top with parsley.

**20**  Remove the baking tray of potatoes from the oven – *be careful*. Lift each potato from the tray with a folded teacloth and put it into the vegetable dish.

**21**  The meal is now ready.

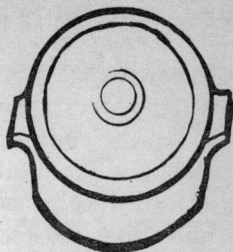

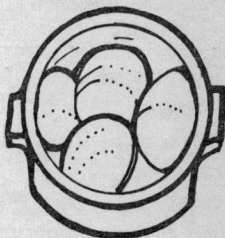

# Sweet and sour pork

The mixture of sweet and sour flavours given in the recipe below is associated with Chinese cooking. This dish is not difficult to make; you will find ingredients like bean sprouts and soy sauce in supermarkets. Ask the butcher to slice the meat for you or get a grown-up to do this.

**You will need:**

| | |
|---|---|
| *small onion* | 1 |
| *lean pork, cut into 1.5 cm (½ inch) slices* | 450 grammes (1 lb) |
| *olive oil or corn oil or frying oil* | 1 tablespoon |
| *cornflour* | 2 level teaspoons |
| *pineapple cubes* | 1 small can |
| *vinegar* | 1 tablespoon |
| *water, see stage 6* | |
| *soy sauce* | 1 tablespoon |
| *brown sugar* | 1 tablespoon |
| *salt* | pinch |
| *pepper* | shake |
| *bean sprouts* | 1 small can or about 100 grammes (4 oz) fresh sprouts |

*These ingredients will make 4 servings.*

**You will use:**
plates for ingredients, chopping board, small sharp knife, larger sharp knife, tablespoon, wok, teaspoon, basin, can opener, wooden spoon, measure, serving dish.

**For success:**
Do not over-cook the dish after adding the pineapple and bean sprouts.

**1** Peel and finely chop the onion or ask a grown-up to do this for you.

**2** Cut the sliced pork into neat 1.5 cm (½ inch) pieces.

**3** Measure the oil and pour it into the wok. As the picture shows, this is a special shaped pan, see the *Note!* at the end of the recipe.

**4** Put the cornflour into the basin.

**5** Pierce 2 holes in the can of pineapple or get a grown-up to do this for you.

**6** Pour the syrup from the can of pineapple into the measure, add the vinegar and check the amount of liquid; you should have 284 ml (½ pint). If you do not have sufficient add water to make up the quantity.

**7** Pour this liquid over the cornflour, stirring well to blend, add the soy sauce and brown sugar.

**8** Open the can of pineapple, see also stage 15.

**9** Light the gas burner or switch on the electric hotplate.

**10** Place the wok over the heat and leave for about 1 minute, make sure the heat is set to moderate only.

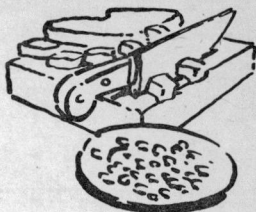

**11** Add the pork to the wok and fry in the oil for 5 minutes, stir well to prevent the meat becoming too brown, but pork must be well-cooked.

**12** Add the onion to the pork and cook for 2 minutes.

**13** Give the cornflour mixture a very good stir and pour this into the wok.

**14** Stir well as the mixture comes to the boil and thickens, then add the salt and pepper; taste the sauce (allow it to cool slightly) and make sure you have the right amount of flavour.

**15** Add the pineapple cubes and heat for 1 minute; open the can of bean sprouts, drain these.

**16** Add the bean sprouts and heat for another 1 minute then serve the dish. It can be served with vegetables or with cooked rice, see pages 116–17.

*Note!* A wok can be used for frying other foods. It is particularly good when you do not want the food to become over-cooked.

## To make a change

This dish looks very attractive if you add a diced green pepper to the sauce after it has thickened and before adding the pineapple cubes. On page 91 you will find directions for preparing a green pepper, see stages 3–5.

Instead of using pork you could use portions of frying chicken. Because these are very lean you will need to increase the oil to 2 tablespoons. It looks very like a Chinese dish if you ask a grown-up to cut the flesh away from the chicken bones and cut this into neat dice. The cooking time will then be similar to the pork.

## Bean sprouts

Bean sprouts are delicious in salads, particularly if you buy fresh sprouts. Greengrocers and vegetable departments of supermarkeets will sell them. You can also cook them as a vegetable to go with other foods. Allow 1 minute cooking time in boiling salted water so the sprouts retain their crisp texture. Canned bean sprouts should be drained very well when using them in a salad or for cooking.

# Cooking rice

It is important to choose the right kind of rice. When you make a rice pudding buy short grain rice (often called 'round' or 'pudding' or 'Carolina' rice). For savoury dishes buy long grain rice (it is sometimes called 'Patna' rice).

There are many ways of cooking long grain rice but the following method is the easiest and one of the best.

**1** To cook long grain rice for 4 people fill a 284 ml (½ pint or 10 fl oz) cup with rice. Put it into a saucepan.

**2** Fill the cup twice with cold water, i.e. 2 x 284 ml (2 x ½ pint or 2 x 10 fl oz) cups and pour this over the rice.

**3** Add 1 *level* teaspoon salt.

**4** Light the gas burner or switch on the electric hotplate.

**5** Heat the water and rice quickly, stir with a fork.

**6** Cover the saucepan with a lid; turn the heat down to low.

**7** Simmer the rice for 15 minutes. At the end of this time the rice should be tender and the water all absorbed, so you just lift the rice grains with a fork to make it fluffy, then spoon it out of the saucepan and arrange it around the sweet and sour pork.

## To make a change

Add 1–2 tablespoons chopped parsley to the cooked rice.

# Rice salad

Cook extra rice and use this as the basis for a salad. Mix a little mayonnaise or salad dressing with the hot rice, then allow it to cool. You can then add a variety of different vegetables, such as cooked peas, diced cooked carrots or grated raw carrot and chopped celery and chopped tomatoes.

# Leftover rice

Any rice left over can be used in a salad as suggested above. The flavour is not quite as good if you mix cold rice with salad dressing or mayonnaise.

Cover any leftover rice and keep it in the refrigerator. To re-heat the rice put it in a saucepan with enough cold water to cover, bring the water to boiling point then drain the rice through a fine sieve.

Cooked rice can be frozen. Put it into a plastic box or bag. It is a good idea to squeeze the bag when the rice is nearly frozen to separate the grains. If freezing in a box, lift the lid and gently fork the rice before it is completely frozen and hard.

# Did you know?

There are two ways to separate egg whites from yolks:

**1** Have a saucer ready.

**a** Crack the egg gently on the edge of a cup or saucer, then pull the halves of the egg apart carefully and allow the egg to drop on to the saucer.
**b** Put an egg cup over the yolk; holding it firmly, pour the egg white into a basin, then take the egg cup away.

**2** Have two basins or cups ready. Crack the egg gently on the edge of a cup or saucer.

**a** Pull the two halves of the shell apart slightly and allow the white to drop into one basin.
**b** Now open the egg and pour the yolk into the second basin.

If you have let a little egg yolk drop into the white it will not whip properly, so you must take it out. Use the damp corner of a piece of kitchen paper or the corner of a damp, clean teacloth, or use one half of the egg shell – all these are better than using a teaspoon.

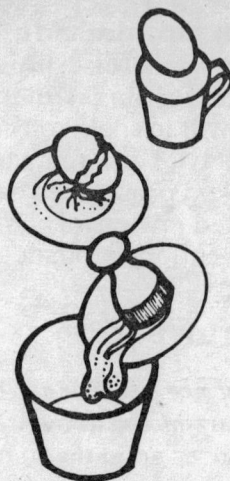

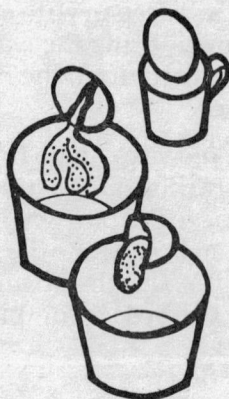

# Yeast cookery

Yeast cookery is fun because yeast is a living substance that makes your flour mixture rise and grow.

Yeast cookery is not difficult, but here are some things to remember:

If you use fresh yeast make sure it is quite fresh. It should be fairly soft and crumble easily. Keep the yeast well wrapped and store it in the refrigerator until you are ready to use it. If you cannot buy fresh yeast (health food stores generally stock it), buy dried yeast. The recipes tell you about using both fresh and dried yeast.

You will see that the yeast mixture is left to 'prove' – which is another word for 'rise' – and you do this by leaving the yeast in the warm room. Do not put the dough into the oven or anywhere too hot; if you do you will spoil the mixture because you will destroy the yeast too soon.

The recipes tell you to 'knead' the dough; do not do this too roughly or for too long a period. Stage 10 of the bread recipe on page 122 shows how to tell whether you have kneaded for a sufficiently long time.

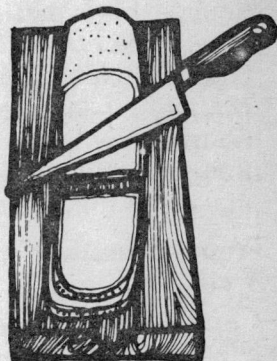

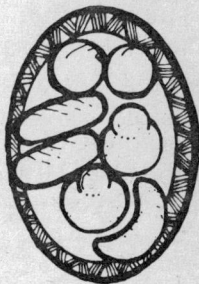

## ade bread

...made loaf of bread is delicious ...eat treat for the whole family. As you will see the recipe states 'strong' flour as this is particularly good for yeast cookery. You can buy it at grocers and health food shops, but if you cannot find any use ordinary plain flour. You will not need self-raising flour or baking powder as the yeast makes the mixture rise.

### You will need:

| | |
|---|---|
| *fresh yeast* | 15 grammes (½ oz)– do not use any |
| *or* | more |
| *dried yeast* | 2 *level* teaspoons |
| *water* | 284 ml (½ pint) |
| *sugar\** | 1 teaspoon |
| *strong white flour* | 450 grammes (1 lb) |
| *salt* | 1 *level* teaspoon |
| *milk* | about 1 tablespoon |

*These ingredients will make 1 loaf.*

### You will use:

plates for ingredients, basin, teaspoon, flat-bladed knife, saucepan or kettle, measuring jug, wooden spoon, sieve, mixing bowl, pastry board, flour dredger, piece of polythene or clean teacloth, 1 kg (2 lb) loaf tin, pastry brush, wire cooling tray.

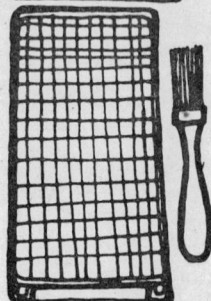

## For success:

Read page 119 again; follow all directions carefully. Do not try and hurry the process of making bread, just leave the dough to rise while you do other jobs.

**1** *If using fresh yeast* put this into the basin and cream with a teaspoon until the yeast becomes quite liquid.*

**2** Light the gas burner or switch on the electric hotplate or kettle.

**3** Heat some water in a saucepan or kettle until it is just at blood heat – this means it will feel slightly warm. Do not make it too hot. Pour enough into the measuring jug to give 284 ml (½ pint).

**4** Pour *most* of the water over the fresh yeast, save just a little of the water. Stir with a wooden spoon.

**5** *If using dried yeast*, heat the water as in stage 3 and pour 284 ml (½ pint) into the measuring jug; then pour most of the water into the basin.

**6** Add the sugar, stir well, then sprinkle the dried yeast on top of the water; wait 10 minutes, then stir again.

**7** *If using either fresh or dried yeast*, sprinkle a very little flour over the top of the yeast mixture and leave for about

*Until recently fresh yeast was creamed with sugar. Nowadays it has been found that it is better to avoid the sugar at stage 1. If you *do* want to cream the yeast with sugar it will not spoil the bread but it is not necessary.

Instead of using sugar at stages 1 and 5 you could use a teaspoon of honey.

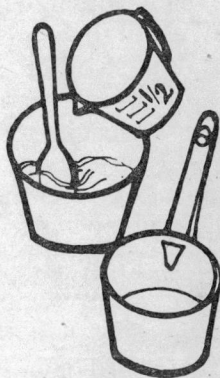

15 minutes or until the surface is covered with little bubbles.

**8** Sieve the flour and salt into the mixing bowl, then make a hollow in the centre of the flour and pour the yeast mixture into this. Mix everything together with the wooden spoon; then put this down and use your hands or a flat-bladed knife.

**9** Gather the dough together to make a *soft ball*. You may find you need to add the rest of the water – remember you did not use quite all the 284 ml (½ pint). It is a good idea not to make the yeast dough too wet to begin with, for different makes of flour vary in the amount of water they need. If the dough is too wet, use a generous amount of flour on the pastry board when kneading.

**10** Put the ball of dough on to the pastry board or working surface. Shake over a little flour, from the flour dredger, then knead with your hands until smooth. *Kneading* is done by pulling the dough gently, then folding it back again – pulling, folding all the time. *To test the dough:* Dip your finger in a little flour, then press it into the dough; if insufficiently kneaded you will make a mark which does not come out. When you have kneaded enough the mark comes out slowly.

**11** Put the kneaded dough back into the bowl and cover with a piece of polythene or a clean teacloth.

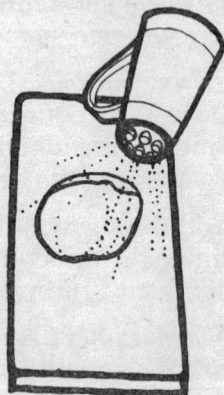

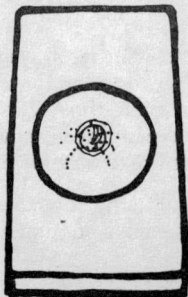

**12** Leave in a warm room (not in a draught) or in the airing cupboard for about 1 hour, until it has risen to twice the size it was at stage 11 – do not let dough rise more than this.

**13** Lift the dough from the bowl on to the pastry board, add a shake of flour, knead once more as described in stage 10.

**14** If you are making your loaf in a tin, press out the dough to a neat oblong. A–B should be the length of the loaf tin and A–C and B–D should be about three times the width of the loaf tin.

*Note!* If you wish to make a different shaped loaf, see page 126.

**15** Fold the dough in three so you have a shape the same size as the tin. While you are doing this put the loaf tin in a warm place. Grease the tin with oil or melted fat.

**16** Put the folded dough into the tin; press down *gently*.

**17** Set your oven at hot, 425°F, 220°C or gas mark 7.

**18** Brush the top of the dough with the milk; cover the top of the tin very lightly with a piece of polythene or a cloth.

**19** Leave the tin in a warm place for about 20 minutes to allow the yeast dough to rise again up the tin. You can remove the polythene or cloth towards the end of this period so that it does not touch the dough.

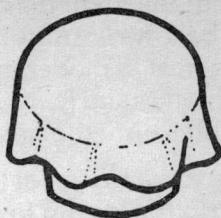

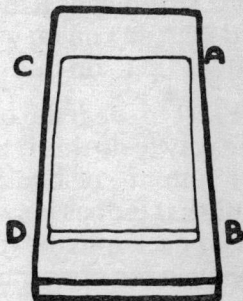

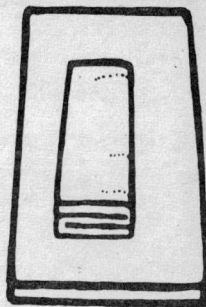

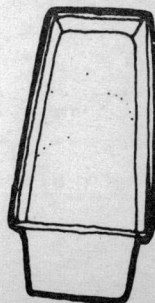

**20** Put the tin in the centre of the oven and bake for 15 minutes, then lower the oven heat to moderate, 350°F, 180°C or gas mark 4 and leave for another 15–20 minutes until the bread looks brown.

**21** Lift the tin out of the oven *carefully* and tip the loaf on to a wire cooling tray. This means handling the hot tin and loaf, so you may prefer to ask a grown-up to do this for you.

**22** Test to see if the bread is cooked. The way to do this is to tap the bread on the bottom – it should give a 'hollow' sound; if it does not do so, put the bread back into the tin and cook it in the oven for a few more minutes.

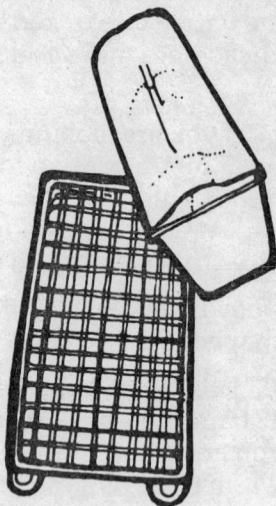

**Milk bread**. Use milk instead of water to mix the dough. Heat this as stage 3 on page 122.

**Fruit bread**. Use the recipe as page 120, but add 100 grammes (4 oz) dried fruit, such as sultanas or currants or seedless raisins or mixed fruit at stage 8, page 122.

**Brown bread.** Instead of using all strong white flour as in the recipe that begins on page 120, use half strong white and half strong wholemeal flour. You may find you need a very little extra water at stage 9, page 122, and that the bread takes a few minutes longer to cook.

**Wholemeal bread.** Instead of using strong white flour use strong wholemeal or wheatmeal flour or stoneground flour. Stoneground describes a method of grinding the wheat to make flour. This flour absorbs more liquid so use a generous 284 ml ($\frac{1}{2}$ pint) water. The loaf will take at least 5 minutes longer cooking time.

**Richer breads.** In all the bread doughs above and the basic bread you can add $\frac{1}{2}$ tablespoon olive or corn oil to the water at stage 4, page 121, or rub in 15 grammes ($\frac{1}{2}$ oz) lard or margarine at stage 8, on page 122, before adding the yeast liquid.

## Different shapes for bread

There are many shapes for bread and you will enjoy making these. Here is one you can try.

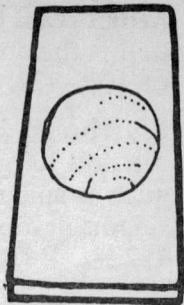

## Cottage loaf

**1** Follow the recipe for bread from page 120 to stage 13 on page 123.

**2** Make two-thirds of the dough into a round at stage 16.

**3** Put this on to a greased warm flat baking tray and flatten it a little on top.

**4** Make the rest of the dough into a smaller round and put this on top of the bigger round.

**5** Press your floured finger in the middle of the top round.

**6** Brush the bread with milk and leave to 'prove' (rise) in a warm place for 15–20 minutes.

**7** Bake as the tin loaf (stages 20–2, page 124).

# Rolls

**1** If you know how to make the basic yeast dough as in the home-made bread on pages 120–24, you can also make small rolls, which would be splendid for a picnic or a party.

**2** You can make white or milk or brown or wholemeal rolls.

**3** Follow the recipe for the home-made bread right up to stage 10 on page 122.

**4** Put the dough on to the pastry board and cut it into 16–20 small pieces. Now form each piece into the shape you want. The pictures below show some of the shapes you can make.

Small rounds

Small cottage loaves

Crescent shapes – these are sometimes called horse-shoe rolls.

Straight rolls (called batons) – mark these on top with a knife to make them look interesting.

**5** Set your oven at hot to very hot, 425–450°F, 220–230°C or gas mark 7–8.

**6** Lift the shapes on to 2 warmed greased baking trays. Remember that they will rise and spread out as they 'prove', so do not put too many on the same tray and do not put them too close

to one another. You can brush the rolls with milk if you wish, but if you like them to be very crisp I would not do this.

**7** Allow the rolls to 'prove' in a warm place for 10–15 minutes, until they are nearly twice the size they were at stage 6.

**8** Bake the rolls just above the centre of the oven for approximately 12 minutes, until they are golden brown in colour. You will probably find the rolls on the baking tray nearer the top of the oven cook a little before the ones on the lower tray.

**9** Take the trays out of the oven *carefully* and lift the rolls on to a wire cooling tray.

*Note!* Bread keeps well for several days, but rolls are nicer if they are eaten the day they are baked, or if you warm them for a few minutes if they have become a little stale.

You can freeze the rolls when baked. Cool, then pack into polythene boxes and freeze.

# Hot cross buns

These home-made buns will be appreciated by your family on Good Friday. Make them the day before and just warm them in the oven, to serve for breakfast, or bake the buns, allow to cool and freeze them. As this recipe uses more sugar, fruit and some fat you use 15 grammes (½ oz) yeast to only 350 grammes (12 oz) flour, whereas with bread 15 grammes (½ oz) will raise 450 grammes (1 lb) flour.

## You will need:

| | |
|---|---|
| *fresh yeast* | 15 grammes (½ oz) – be generous with this |
| *or* | |
| *dried yeast* | 2 *level* teaspoons |
| *sugar* | 50 grammes (2 oz) |
| *water* | 4 tablespoons |
| *milk* | 142 ml (¼ pint) |
| *strong white flour* | 350 grammes (12 oz) |
| *salt* | pinch |
| *mixed spice* | ½ teaspoon |
| *ground cinnamon* | ½–1 teaspoon |
| *margarine* | 50 grammes (2 oz) |
| *mixed dried fruit (raisins, sultanas, currants)* | 75–100 grammes (3–4 oz) |
| to glaze: | |
| *sugar* | 50 grammes (2 oz) |
| *water* | 2 tablespoons |

*These ingredients will make 12–16 buns.*

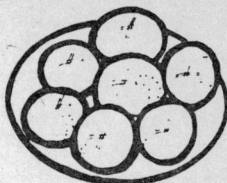

**You will use:**
plates for ingredients, basin, teaspoon, measuring jug, saucepan, wooden spoon, sieve, mixing bowl, flat-bladed knife, pastry board, flour dredger, piece of polythene or clean teacloth, 2 baking trays, sharp knife, small basin or cup, pastry brush, wire cooling tray.

**For success:**
Follow the advice on yeast cookery given on page 119.

1 *If using fresh yeast*, put into the basin and cream this.

2 Light the gas burner or switch on the electric hotplate.

3 Heat the water and milk together in a saucepan until they just reach blood heat. This means the liquid will feel slightly warm – do not make it too hot. Pour the liquid over the yeast and sugar, and stir with a wooden spoon.

4 *If using dried yeast*, heat the water and milk as in stage 3 and pour it into the basin.

5 Add a teaspoon of the sugar, stir well, sprinkle the dried yeast on top of the liquid, wait for 10 minutes, then stir again.

6 *If using fresh or dried yeast*, sprinkle a little flour over the top of the yeast mixture and leave for about 15 minutes, or until you see the surface is covered with little bubbles.

**7** Sieve the flour, salt, mixed spice and ground cinnamon into the mixing bowl.

**8** Add the margarine to the bowl, and rub this into the flour mixture until it looks like fine breadcrumbs.

**9** Add the rest of the sugar and the mixed dried fruit, then make a well in the centre of the flour mixture and pour the yeast mixture into this.

**10** Mix everything together with the wooden spoon, then put this down and use a flat-bladed knife or your hands.

**11** Gather the dough together to make a smooth *soft ball*. See comments on stage 9, page 122.

**12** Knead the dough until smooth as stage 10 on page 122. Put the dough back into the mixing bowl, cover it with a piece of polythene or a clean teacloth and leave in a warm place for about 1¼–1½ hours, until it has risen to *just* twice the size. Bun dough takes longer to rise than bread dough, for the mixture is heavier.

**13** Lift the dough from the bowl on to the pastry board again, add a shake of flour and knead again until smooth.

**14** Put 2 flat baking trays in a warm place, grease them lightly, see page 9.

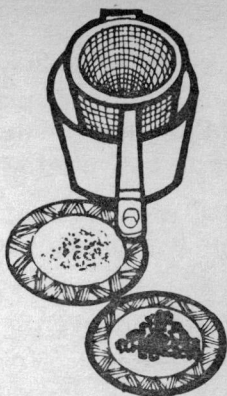

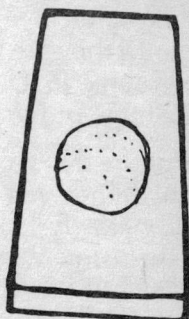

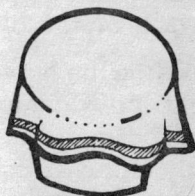

**15** Cut the dough into about 12–16 pieces. Roll each piece into a neat ball and put these on to the trays, leave spaces between the balls.

**16** Flatten the buns slightly and mark an X (cross) in the centre of each with a knife.

**17** Set your oven to hot, 425°F, 220°C or gas mark 7.

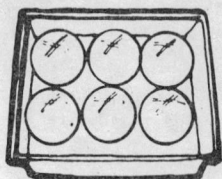

**18** Leave the buns in the room or airing cupboard for 15 minutes to 'prove', i.e. rise until they are nearly twice their size at stage 16. Do not cover the buns while they 'prove'.

**19** Put the trays of buns just above the centre of the oven and bake for approximately 15 minutes until the buns are brown; you will probably find that the buns on the baking tray nearer the top of the oven cook a little before the ones on the lower tray.

**20** While the buns are cooking put the sugar and water for the glaze into a small basin or cup. When the buns are ready remove from the oven and dip the pastry brush into the glaze and brush the buns with this, to give them a shine.

**21** Lift the buns off the baking trays on to the wire cooling tray to cool.

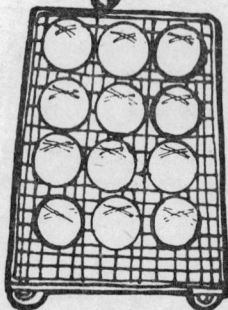

# Fruit buns

Follow the directions for making hot cross buns on pages 129–32, and use the same ingredients but *leave out* the mixed spice and ground cinnamon and do not mark the X (cross) on the buns.

# Bath buns

1 Use the same ingredients as for hot cross buns, but leave out the water and the mixed spice and ground cinnamon.

2 Mix the buns to stage 9, then add 2 eggs (these take the place of the water).

3 Continue the recipe to stage 16.

4 Put the balls on to the warmed greased baking trays and flatten slightly.

5 Take 6–8 lumps of sugar and put these on to a piece of greaseproof paper.

6 Crush the lumps of sugar very lightly with a rolling pin, so you have small pieces of sugar.

7 Brush the top of the buns with a little milk. Sprinkle over the pieces of sugar.

8 Continue as in stages 18 to 19, page 132. Do not use the sugar and water glaze.

9 Lift the buns off the baking trays on to a wire cooling tray to cool.

# Interesting puddings and desserts

## Orange upside down cake

Although this is called a cake, it makes a delicious pudding and on page 137 is the recipe for a sauce to serve with it. You can serve this dish for tea or for a party dish without the sauce. Use jellied marmalade if possible, rather than the thick-cut type.

**You will need:**
for the glaze:

| | |
|---|---|
| *butter or margarine* | 25 grammes (1 oz) |
| *jelly marmalade* | 3 tablespoons |
| *mandarin oranges* | 1 medium can |

for the cake:

| | |
|---|---|
| *margarine* | 100 grammes (4 oz) |
| *caster sugar* | 100 grammes (4 oz) |
| *eggs* | 2 |
| *self-raising flour (or plain flour and 1½ level teaspoons baking powder)* | 150 grammes (6 oz) |
| *milk* | 1 tablespoon |

*These ingredients will make 6–8 slices.*

**You will use:**
plates for ingredients, flat-bladed knife, 18 cm (7 inch) cake tin (*without a loose base*) or round or square oven-proof dish, tablespoon, can opener, jug, mixing bowl, wooden spoon, cup, sieve, large serving plate.

**For success:**
Follow the directions for creaming on page 172 and test the cake carefully at stage 14. Page 138 tells you about testing cakes.

**1** Set your oven to very moderate, 325°F, 160°C or gas mark 3.

**2** Spread most of the butter or margarine at the bottom of the cake tin or oven-proof dish, and a little round the sides of the tin or dish.

**3** Put the marmalade at the bottom of the tin, and spread it out evenly.

**4** Make 2 holes in the can of mandarin oranges. This is not easy to do, so it would be a good idea to ask a grown-up to help you.

**5** Pour the liquid from the can into the jug, then open the can properly.

**6** Tip the orange segments into the tin or dish and spread evenly over the marmalade.

**7** Put the margarine and sugar into the mixing bowl.

**8** Cream with the wooden spoon until soft and light, see page 172.

**9** Break the first egg into a cup, then add to the margarine and sugar, and beat well.

**10** Break the second egg into a cup, then add to the margarine and sugar, and beat well.

**11** Sieve the self-raising flour (or plain flour and baking powder) into the mixing bowl, then blend into the margarine mixture with an ordinary tablespoon.

**12** Lastly, add the milk and mix gently but thoroughly.

See the note on page 172 about how you can cream margarine and sugar very quickly if using the modern soft margarines.

**13** Spoon the cake mixture on top of the oranges, scrape the bowl clean, and smooth the mixture very flat on top.

**14** Bake for 1¼ hours in the middle of a very moderate oven until firm to the touch; page 138 tells you about testing cakes.

**15** Take out of the oven *carefully* and let it stand for 3 minutes.

**16** Have the large serving plate ready and tip the cake upside down on to this.

**17** Serve hot or cold, either by itself or with the orange sauce or with ice-cream.

# Orange sauce

The sauce is not only very good with the orange upside down cake, but with ice cream. You can serve it hot or cold.

**You will need:**

| | |
|---|---|
| *syrup* | from the canned mandarin organes |
| *orange marmalade* | 2 tablespoons |
| *orange* | 1 |
| *cornflour or arrowroot* | 2 *level* teaspoons |

*These ingredients will make 6–8 servings.*

**You will use:**
jug, saucepan, tablespoon, sharp knife, chopping board, lemon squeezer, basin, teaspoon, wooden spoon, sauce boat.

**For success:**
Stir well as the sauce thickens.

**1** Pour the syrup from the jug into the saucepan.

**2** Add the marmalade.

**3** Cut the orange into halves and squeeze out the juice.

**4** Put the cornflour or arrowroot into the basin and blend with the orange juice.

**5** Tip this into the saucepan.

**6** Light the gas burner or switch on the electric hotplate and turn the heat low.

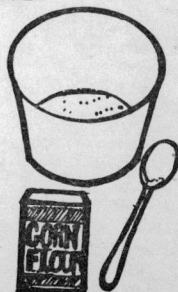

**7** Stir all the time as the sauce thickens and becomes smooth.

**8** Pour into a sauce boat and serve hot or cold.

## To make a change

**Cherry upside down cake.** Use a medium can of stoned cherries for the cake instead of the oranges and redcurrant jelly instead of jelly marmalade. Use the syrup from the cherries and redcurrant jelly instead of marmalade in the sauce.

## Testing cakes

**1** See if the cake has shrunk away from the sides of the tin.

**2** Press firmly on top. If your finger leaves a mark the cake is not done.

**3** Tip the tin carefully over the wire cooling tray or plate. A grown-up should help you do this. Some cakes should be allowed to cool in the tin in which they were baked. This applies to very rich fruit cakes or gingerbreads that are full of black treacle.

# Ginger pear upside down cake

This is another excellent pudding or cake. It has pears at the bottom and a ginger-flavoured cake. On page 143 is a ginger sauce to serve with it. Upside down cakes are very popular in America.

**You will need:**
for the glaze:

| | |
|---|---|
| *margarine* | 25 grammes (1 oz) |
| *golden syrup* | 2 tablespoons |
| *canned pear halves* | 6–8 |

for the cake:

| | |
|---|---|
| *margarine* | 100 grammes (4 oz) |
| *caster sugar* | 100 grammes (4 oz) |
| *eggs* | 2 |
| *self-raising flour (or plain flour and 1½ level teaspoons baking powder)* | 150 grammes (6 oz) |
| *ground ginger* | 1–2 teaspoons |
| *milk* | 1 tablespoon |

*These ingredients will make 6–8 slices.*

**You will use:**
plates for ingredients, flat-bladed knife, 18 cm (7 inch) cake tin (*without a loose base*) or round or square oven-proof dish, tablespoon, can opener, jug, mixing bowl, wooden spoon, cup, sieve, teaspoon, large serving plate.

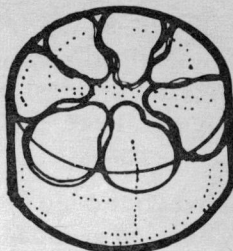

**For success:**
Follow the directions for creaming on page 172 and test the cake carefully at stage 15. Page 138 tells you about testing cakes.

**1** Set your oven to very moderate, 325°F, 160°C or gas mark 3.

**2** Spread most of the margarine at the bottom of the cake tin or oven-proof dish, and a little round the sides of the tin or dish.

**3** Put the golden syrup at the bottom of the tin.

**4** Make 2 holes in the can of halved pears. This is not an easy thing to do, so it would be a good idea to ask a grown-up to help you.

**5** Pour all the liquid from the can into the jug, then spoon 1 tablespoon of this liquid over the golden syrup.

**6** Open the can of pears properly and lift out the pears.

**7** Arrange 6–8 halves in a neat design over the golden syrup and tablespoon of liquid from the can.

**8** Put the margarine and sugar into the mixing bowl.

**9** Cream with the wooden spoon until soft and light (see page 172).

**10** Break the first egg into a cup, then add to the margarine and sugar, and beat well.

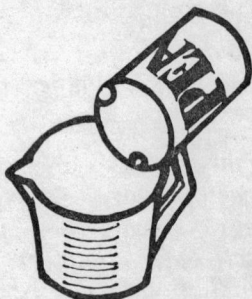

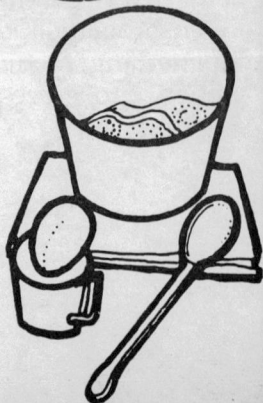

**11** Break the second egg into a cup, then add to the margarine and sugar, and beat well.

**12** Sieve the flour (or flour and baking powder) and ground ginger into the mixing bowl, then blend into the margarine mixture with an ordinary tablespoon.

**13** Lastly, add the milk and mix gently but thoroughly.

See the note on page 172 about how you can cream margarine and sugar very quickly if using the modern soft margarines.

**14** Spoon the cake mixture on top of the pears, scrape the bowl clean, and smooth the mixture very flat on top.

**15** Bake for $1\frac{1}{4}$ hours in the middle of a very moderate oven until firm to the touch; page 138 tells you about testing cakes.

**16** Take out of the oven *carefully*, and let it stand for 3 minutes.

**17** Have the large serving plate ready and tip the cake upside down on to this.

**18** Serve hot or cold, either by itself or with the ginger sauce or with ice cream.

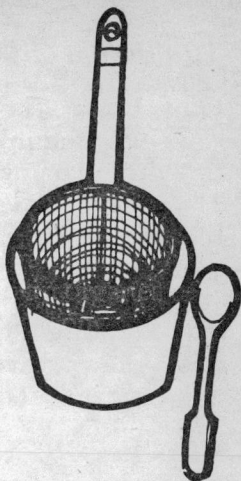

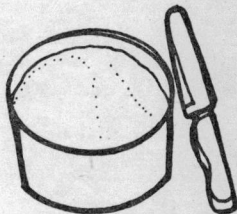

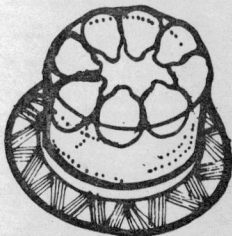

## To make a change

**Ginger cake.** The mixture for the cake can be cooked in a 15 cm (6 inch) cake tin without using the pears and glaze. The cooking time will be shorter than the time given in stage 15. Allow just 1 hour at a very moderate heat, 325°F, 160°C or gas mark 3. Turn the cake out of the tin carefully on to a wire cooling tray. Allow to cool then shake a little icing sugar over the cake through a fine sieve.

# Ginger sauce

This sauce is very good poured over ice cream as well.

**You will need:**

| | |
|---|---|
| *golden syrup* | 2 tablespoons |
| *preserved or crystallized ginger* | 50 grammes (2 oz) |
| *cornflour or arrowroot* | 2 *level* teaspoons |
| *water** | 284 ml (½ pint) |

*These ingredients will make 6–8 servings.*

**You will use:**
tablespoon, saucepan, chopping board, sharp knife, basin, teaspoon, measuring jug, wooden spoon, sauce boat.

**For success:**
Stir well as the sauce thickens.

**1** Put the golden syrup into the saucepan.

**2** Put the preserved or crystallized ginger on a chopping board and cut it into small pieces, tip the ginger into the saucepan.

**3** Put the cornflour or arrowroot into the basin and blend with the water.

**4** Pour into the saucepan.

* Or use the liquid from the canned pears (in the ginger pear upside down cake). As this is rather sweet use only 1 tablespoon golden syrup.

**5** Light the gas burner or switch on the electric hotplate and turn the heat low.

**6** Stir all the time as the sauce thickens and becomes smooth.

**7** Pour into a sauce boat and serve hot or cold.

## Another way to use the ginger sauce

This ginger sauce is delicious if served with melon to make a pudding.

Halve small melons and take out the seeds from the middle, discard these.

Cut a large melon into thick slices or ask a grown-up to do this for you and then remove the seeds.

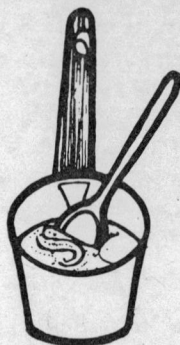

# Caramelled rice pudding

The caramel topping makes this rice pudding very interesting. If you have not time to cook the pudding, open a can of creamed rice, tip it into a pie dish and warm it for about 20 minutes in the oven, then add the sugar topping.

**You will need:**
for the pudding:
*round (often called short grain Carolina) rice*                    2 tablespoons
*caster or granulated sugar*                       1–2 tablespoons
*milk*                              584 ml (1 pint)
*butter (optional)*            small knob

for the sugar topping:
*brown sugar*                    2–3 tablespoons

*These ingredients will make 4 servings.*

**You will use:**
plates for ingredients, 1 litre (1½–2 pint) pie dish, tablespoon, measure for milk (although this can be poured from the bottle or carton), flat-bladed knife.

**For success:**
Cook a rice pudding, or any other milk puddings you make, as slowly as possible in the oven.

**1** Set your oven at slow to very slow, 275–300°F, 140–150°C or gas mark 1–2.

**2** Put the rice, caster or granulated sugar and milk into the pie dish. It is a good idea to add the small piece of butter, for that gives a more creamy pudding; but a piece of suet or margarine could be used instead.

**3** Put the pudding into the centre of the oven and let it cook for about 2 hours, or follow the instructions given under 'To make a change' below.

**4** When the pudding is almost ready to serve take it out of the oven *carefully*; be careful where you put it down – the pie dish can crack if it is put on a damp surface.

**5** Sprinkle enough brown sugar over the top to give a good coating and put the pudding back again in the oven, but place the dish nearer the top of the oven, so the sugar makes a moist brown topping.

## To make a change

Have you tried adding dried fruit to a rice pudding?

Put 2–3 tablespoons of sultanas or seedless raisins into the pie dish at stage 2.

## To save fuel

It wastes heat if you use the oven just for a pudding, so you could bake *large* jacket potatoes. Page 109 tells you how to prepare these. They will take the same time as the pudding, if placed near the centre of the oven.

You can cook the rice pudding (and jacket potatoes) rather more quickly, i.e. in a moderate oven, 325-350°F, 160-180°C, or gas mark 3-4. This means that when you make the hunter's chicken casserole (page 108), you can put the rice pudding into the oven about 30 minutes before the casserole. Cook the pudding towards the bottom of the oven.

# Cherry tarts

Make sure the pastry is baked until crisp, and allow it and the glaze (see recipe) to cool before you fill the tarts.

**You will need:**
for the pastry:
| | |
|---|---|
| *flour, preferably plain* | 100 grammes (4 oz) |
| *salt* | pinch |
| *margarine or butter or cooking fat* | 50 grammes (2 oz) |
| *egg yolk* | 1 |
| *water* | nearly 1 tablespoon |

for the filling:
| | |
|---|---|
| *cherries (stoned)* | 1 medium can |
| *redcurrant jelly* | 2 tablespoons |
| *arrowroot or cornflour* | 1 *el* teaspoon |

*These ingredients will make 9–12 tarts; if using the metric measurements you have a smaller quantity.*

**You will use:**
plates for ingredients, sieve, mixing bowl, tablespoon, flat-bladed knife, flour dredger, pastry board, rolling pin, 5–8 cm (2–3 inch) pastry cutter, 9 fairly large or 12 smaller patty tins, fork, wire cooling tray, can opener, measuring jug, saucepan, teaspoon, basin, wooden spoon, pastry brush (optional), serving dish.

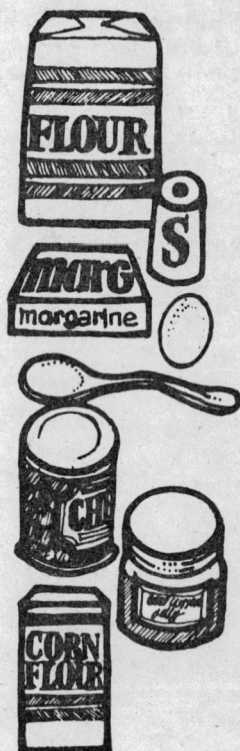

**For success:**
Do not make the pastry dough too damp at stage 4.
Stir the glaze carefully over a *low* heat as it thickens.

**1** Do not heat the oven too early as it takes time to make pastry.

**2** Sieve the flour and salt into the mixing bowl, add the margarine, butter or cooking fat.

**3** Rub the fat into the flour with the tips of your fingers until the mixture looks like fine breadcrumbs; do not handle the mixture too much.

**4** Add the egg yolk, then gradually add enough water to make the mixture bind together in a ball. You will find you can mix the ingredients with a flat-bladed knife, but it is better to use your finger tips to gather the dough into a ball.

**5** Set your oven to hot, 425°F, 220°C or gas mark 7.

**6** Shake a little flour on to the pastry board, then put the pastry dough on it.

**7** Shake a little flour over the rolling pin.

**8** Roll the pastry lightly, but firmly, until it makes a neat shape, about 5 mm (¼ inch) in thickness.

**9** Cut out the rounds with a pastry cutter.

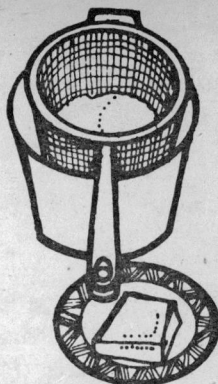

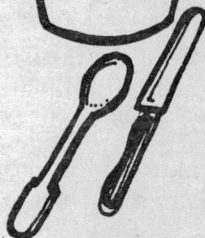

**10** Fit these into some of the patty tins, then gather up the pieces of pastry dough and press them gently together.

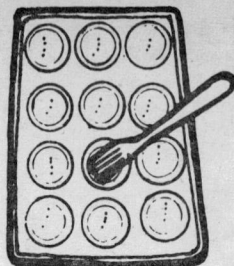

**11** Flour the rolling pin again, roll out the dough as in stage 8, then cut out the rest of the rounds (as in stage 9).

**12** Prick the base of the tart shapes with a fork; this stops them rising, so that they keep a good shape as they are cooked.

**13** Bake for about 12–15 minutes in the centre of the hot oven, check the baking after 8 minutes, lower heat if necessary.

**14** Take the patty tins out of the oven, and let the pastry 'set' for a few minutes; this makes it less likely to break.

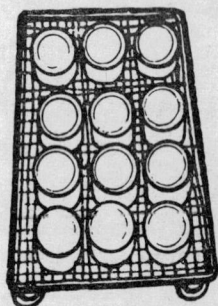

**15** Lift each tart case out of the patty tins very carefully and put on to a wire cooling tray.

**16** Make 2 holes in the can of cherries, or ask a grown-up to do this for you.

**17** Pour a generous 142 ml (¼ pint) of the liquid in the can into the measuring jug; if you have not quite enough add water to give the right quantity.

**18** Now open the can completely and lift out the cherries and put them on to a plate. Make sure you do not add any of the syrup to the cherries; they need to be dry, otherwise they will spoil the crispness of the pastry.

**19** Put the redcurrant jelly into the saucepan.

**20** Put the arrowroot or cornflour into a basin then gradually stir in the 142 ml (¼ pint) liquid; stir all the time as you do this, so the mixture keeps smooth.

**21** Tip this into the saucepan.

**22** Light the gas burner or switch on the electric hotplate and turn the heat low.

**23** Stir the redcurrant jelly mixture with the wooden spoon over the heat until it thickens and turns bright and clear.

**24** Take the pan off the heat and let this mixture begin to cool – it must not be too cold, otherwise it becomes too stiff.

**25** Arrange a few cherries in each tart.

**26** Either spread the redcurrant mixture which is called 'the glaze' over the cherries with a teaspoon or flat-bladed knife or dip the pastry brush into the glaze and brush this over the cherries. Use up all the glaze.

**27** Let the glaze become quite cold, then place the tarts on a serving dish.

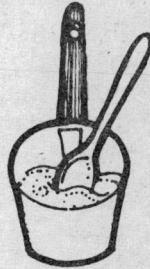

## To make a change

You can use different canned fruit
instead of cherries or use fresh
strawberries.

## A quick way of making pastry

The modern soft (often called luxury)
margarines and vegetable fats soften so
easily today that you can make pastry
without rubbing the fat into the flour.
All you need to do is to put all the
ingredients for the pastry into the
mixing bowl and mix together with a
fork, then continue from stage 5
onwards.

You could use a mixer or food
processor, see pages 14–15.

# Ice-cream

There are many ways of preparing your own ice-cream; this recipe makes a very special kind of ice-cream but it is expensive so I expect you will only have it on special occasions. If you read 'To make a change' on page 155 you will see how to make ice-cream without spending quite so much money.

## You will need:

| | |
|---|---|
| *eggs* | 2 |
| *caster or icing sugar* | about 50 grammes (2 oz) |
| *vanilla essence* | few drops |
| *double cream* | 142 ml (¼ pint) |
| *single cream* | 142 ml (¼ pint) |

*These ingredients will make 4–6 servings.*

## You will use:
plates for ingredients, cup, 2 basins, sieve, wooden spoon, egg whisk, skewer, tablespoon, large freezing tray, serving dishes.

## For success:
Do whisk hard at stage 3 for this makes a very light ice-cream.
Do not over-beat the double cream at stage 5.

**1** Break the first egg into a cup, then tip it into a basin; break the second egg into the cup, then tip this into the basin.

**2** Add the sugar; if you are using icing sugar press this through a sieve with a wooden spoon.

**3** Whisk the eggs and sugar until they are thick; you may want to stop once or twice to have a rest as this is quite hard work and may take a little time. Use a high speed with an electric whisk.

**4** Dip a skewer into the bottle of vanilla essence and let a few drops fall into the mixture; do not add too much.

**5** Pour the double cream into the second basin, whisk until it holds its shape.

**6** Pour in the single cream, mix with the double cream; whisk again until the mixture stands up in soft points.

**7** Spoon the cream into the beaten eggs and sugar; taste the ice-cream and add a little more vanilla essence if necessary.

**8** Spoon it into the freezing tray and freeze it as quickly as possible in the freezing compartment of the refrigerator, or put it into the freezer. It will take at least 1–1½ hours to freeze.

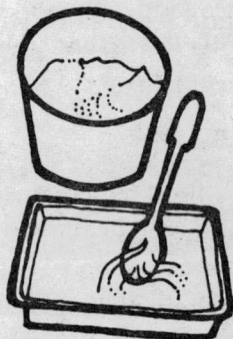

**9** Spoon into the serving dishes.

## To make a change

**Chocolate ice-cream.** Add 1 level tablespoon sieved cocoa or 2 tablespoons chocolate powder at stage 4; you can still use the vanilla essence.

**Coffee ice-cream.** Mix 1 teaspoon instant coffee powder with 1 tablespoon milk and add to the mixture at stage 4; you do not need the vanilla essence.

**Fruit ice-cream.** Rub 225 grammes (8oz) strawberries or raspberries through a sieve or mash them with a fork. Add to the ice-cream at stage 4; you do not need the vanilla essence.

**Cheaper ice-cream.** Use 284 ml (½ pint) unsweetened evaporated milk instead of the double and single cream. Whip this until it is fluffy, see page 170; use instead of the cream at stage 7.

**Custard ice-cream.** Made a thick custard (see the recipe for trifle on page 161 but use only 1 tablespoon custard powder, 284 ml (½ pint) milk). Add 50 grammes (2 oz) caster or sieved icing sugar to the custard. Cover with damp greaseproof paper, so a skin does not form, and allow the custard to cool. Add the custard to the whipped cream or whipped evaporated milk and freeze.

# Sorbets

Refreshing sorbets can be made with fruit juice or fresh or cooked fruit.

**1** Make 425 ml (¾ pint) of fresh orange or grapefruit juice or use the juice from a carton, can or bottle; if unsweetened add 2 tablespoons sugar. You can make 425 ml (¾ pint) fruit pulp by rubbing fresh soft fruit (such as raspberries) through a nylon sieve or putting the fruit into a liquidizer or food processor. Cooked or canned fruit could be used instead; sweeten to taste.

**2** Pour the juice or pulp into a container and place in the freezer or freezing compartment of the refrigerator and freeze until 'mushy', i.e. like thick whipped cream.

**3** Separate the yolks from the whites of 2 eggs. Page 118 tells you how to do this; whisk the whites until stiff. Cover the yolks with 2 tablespoons cold water so they will not dry. You can add the yolks to scrambled eggs or use them instead of 1 whole egg in a pancake batter, see pages 34 and 52.

**4** Remove the frozen fruit juice or purée from the freezer and blend this with the egg whites. Return the mixture to the container and freeze lightly. Eat while freshly made if possible.

*This recipe would serve 4–5 people.*

# Lemon shortbread fingers

These biscuits are delicious with ice cream or to serve at teatime.

**You will need:**

| | |
|---|---|
| *lemon rind* | 1 teaspoon |
| *butter or margarine* | 100 grammes (4 oz) |
| *caster sugar* | 50 grammes (2 oz) |
| *plain flour* | 100 grammes (4 oz) |
| *cornflour* | 50 grammes (2 oz) |

for the topping:
*caster sugar*     1 tablespoon

*These ingredients make about 16 fingers.*

**You will use:**
plates for ingredients, grater, pastry brush, mixing bowl, wooden spoon, sieve, pastry board, rolling pin, flour dredger, knife, 1 or 2 baking trays, 1 tablespoon.

**For success:**
Handle the biscuit dough quite firmly.

**1** To make the lemon rind rub a lemon over the fine side of the grater, be careful not to grate any bitter white pith; use just the yellow part of the lemon rind (called the 'zest'); brush the rind from the grater with a pastry brush.

**2** Put the lemon rind with the butter or margarine and 50 grammes (2 oz) sugar into a mixing bowl.

**3** Beat well until smooth with a wooden spoon or you could use an electric mixer or food processor.

157

**4** Sift the flour and cornflour into the creamed mixture then mix this well with the wooden spoon. You could use an electric mixer or food processor for this stage too.

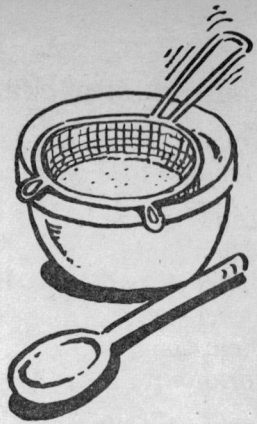

**5** Take the biscuit dough out of the bowl and knead it well. If the dough feels too soft to knead, then all you have to do is to put the dough into a plastic bag and chill it in the refrigerator for 30 minutes.

**6** Set your oven to very moderate, 325°F, 160°C or gas mark 3.

**7** Roll out the dough on a lightly floured board until it is a neat oblong about 23 x 15 cm (9 x 6 inches).

**8** Cut the dough into about 16 fingers and put these on to 1 large or 2 small baking trays (they do not need greasing).

**9** Sprinkle the top of the biscuits with the 1 tablespoon of sugar.

**10** Place the trays of biscuits in the centre of the oven and bake for 15 minutes.

**11** Allow the biscuits to cool on the baking trays then store in an airtight tin.

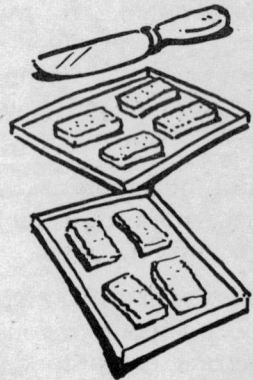

## To make a change

**Chocolate shortbread fingers.** Omit 25 grammes (1 oz) cornflour and use 25 grammes (1 oz) of sweetened chocolate powder (the kind you use when you make a chocolate drink).

**Orange shortbread fingers.** As orange rind has not such a strong flavour as lemon, use 2 teaspoons grated orange rind instead.

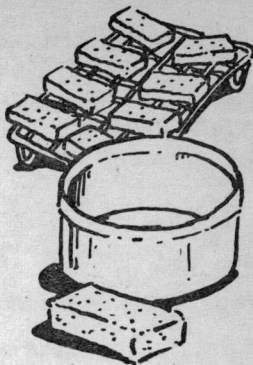

# Fudge walnut sauce

**You will need:**

| | |
|---|---|
| *vanilla fudge* | 100 grammes (4 oz) |
| *top of the milk or* | |
| *single cream* | 2 tablespoons |
| *halved walnuts* | 25–50 grammes |
| | (1–2 oz) |

*These ingredients will make 4–6 servings.*

**You will use:**
double saucepan or basin and saucepan, tablespoon, chopping board, sharp knife, wooden spoon.

**For success:**
Do not over-heat the fudge.

**1** Put the fudge with the creamy milk or cream into the top of the double saucepan or into a basin which fits *safely* over a saucepan.

**2** Put cold water into the bottom of the double saucepan or saucepan.

**3** Light the gas burner or switch on the electric hot plate; turn to moderate.

**4** Leave the fudge mixture until it melts – no longer – then turn off the heat.

**5** Lift the top off the double saucepan or lift the basin out of the water, or ask a grown-up to do this for you, for it must be done *carefully*.

**6** Put the walnuts on to the chopping board and cut them into smaller pieces.

**7** Add these to the melted fudge and stir well; the sauce can be used hot or cold. If you are using the sauce hot, do not pour it over the ice cream until the very last minute.

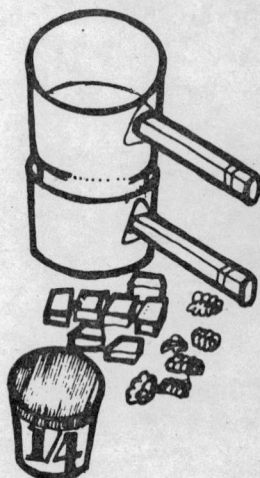

## Ways to serve ice-cream

Ice-cream can be served in many ways:

Top individual portions of jelly with ice-cream.

Serve ice-cream with raw or cooked or canned fruit, or with other puddings.

Top ice-cream with a sauce. Page 137 gives an orange sauce and page 143 a ginger sauce. There is a chocolate sauce in **The Piccolo Cookbook** and a fudge walnut sauce on the opposite page.

Try the orange alaska on page 165.

# Trifle

**You will need:**

| | |
|---|---|
| *trifle sponge cakes* | 3–4 |
| *jam* | 3 tablespoons |

for the custard sauce:

| | |
|---|---|
| *custard powder* | 2 tablespoons |
| *caster or granulated sugar* | 2 tablespoons |
| *milk* | 584 ml (1 pint) |

for decoration:

| | |
|---|---|
| *double cream or whipped evaporated milk* | 3–4 tablespoons |
| *glacé cherries* | about 6 |
| *angelica* | tiny pieces |

*These ingredients will make 4–6 servings.*

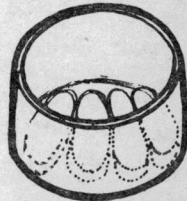

**You will use:**
plates for ingredients, tablespoon, flat-bladed knife, serving dish, basin, saucepan, wooden spoon, egg whisk, teaspoon, sharp knife.

**For success:**
Stir the custard as it thickens to make sure it keeps smooth. *Do not pour too hot custard over the sponge cakes* otherwise you may crack the dish.

1 Split the sponge cakes through the centre, spread with jam, then sandwich them together again and put them into the serving dish.

2 Put the custard powder and sugar into the basin, blend with a little of the milk. Pour the rest of the milk into the saucepan.

3 Light the gas burner or switch on the electric hotplate; heat the milk; watch carefully to see it does not boil over.

4 Pour the very hot milk over the custard, stirring well as you do so.

5 Tip the custard mixture back into the saucepan. Put it back on the burner or hotplate, keeping the heat fairly low.

6 Stir with the wooden spoon as the custard thickens and cook *slowly* for about 5 minutes after it thickens.

7 Allow the custard to cool slightly, stirring once or twice to stop a skin forming, then pour the warm custard over the sponge cakes. Cover the serving dish with a plate and allow the custard to cool.

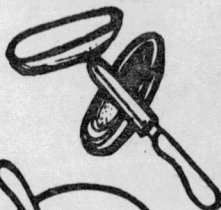

**8** Pour the cream into a basin and whip until it becomes thick or use whipped evaporated milk, see page 170.

**9** Put small teaspoons of cream on top of the custard. Decorate with halved glacé cherries and tiny pieces of angelica.

## To make a change

**Fruit trifle.** Follow stage 1 then top the sponges with fresh soft fruit (like strawberries) or a little canned fruit and syrup from the can; continue as stages 2–9.

**Sherry trifle.** Follow stage 1 then moisten the sponges with 3 tablespoons sweet sherry. Continue as stages 2–9.

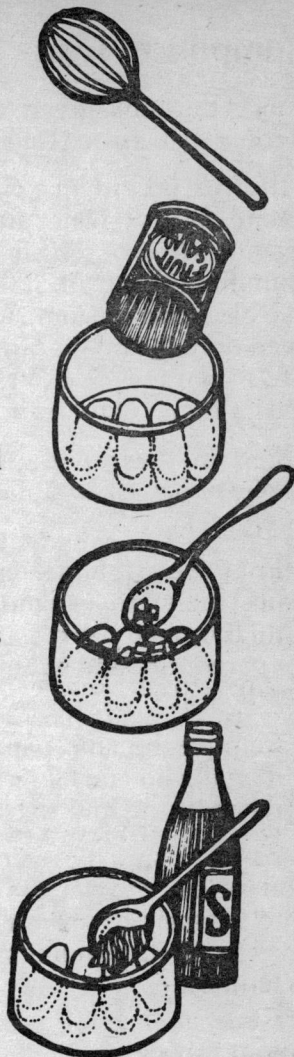

# Compote of fruit

This is the name given to fruit when it is cooked; it is often called stewed fruit.

If the fruit is hard, like plums, you need 284 ml (½ pint) water and 50–75 grammes (2–3 oz) sugar to each 450 grammes (1 lb) fruit. If the fruit is soft, like blackcurrants or raspberries, you need only 142 ml (¼ pint) water and 50–75 grammes (2–3 oz) sugar to each 450 grammes (1 lb) fruit.

**1** Prepare the fruit (e.g. peel and slice apples or halve and stone large apricots or plums).

**2** Put the water and sugar into a saucepan, stir over a moderate heat until the sugar has dissolved. Add the prepared fruit and simmer gently until *nearly tender*.

**3** Remove the saucepan from the heat, put on the lid and allow the fruit to finish cooking in the steam in the pan.

If you are using the oven on a low heat you can put the water, sugar and fruit into a casserole, cover it with a lid and cook for 30–40 minutes or until the fruit is tender.

# Fruit salad

**The Piccolo Cookbook** gives one recipe for fruit salad; another way to prepare this is to cook a mixture of fruits in a compote as above.

# Orange alaska

This dessert is quite a surprise; you have the hot meringue on top of firm cold ice cream. Do time the cooking carefully though, for meringue burns easily in a very hot oven, but, if you have a cooler oven, the ice cream will melt.

**You will need:**

| | |
|---|---|
| *oranges* | 2 very large |
| *caster sugar* | 65 grammes (2½ oz) |
| *egg whites* | 2 |
| *ice cream* | 4 tablespoons |

*These ingredients will make 4 servings.*

**You will use:**
chopping board, sharp knife, teaspoon, basin, plate for sugar, mixing bowl or second basin, egg whisk, large plate, tablespoon, oven-proof dish or plate or tin with a serving plate.

**For success:**
Make sure the egg whites are very stiff and the meringue covers the ice cream.

Make sure the orange halves stand upright when filled.

**1** Set your oven to very hot, 475°F, 240°C or gas mark 8–9.

**2** Cut the oranges in halves across the centre. Remove the pulp with the teaspoon and put into a basin.

**3** Sweeten the pulp with 15 grammes (½ oz) of the sugar and put this back into the halved orange cases.

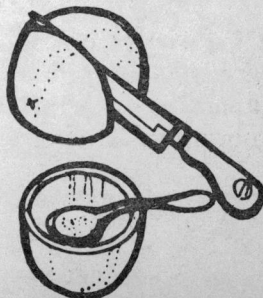

**4** Start to whisk the egg whites (see tips on page 118 for separating egg whites and whisking them) until nearly stiff; cover the bowl with a plate so they do not become liquid again.

**5** Put the ice cream on top of the orange pulp.

**6** Continue whisking the egg whites until they are very stiff.

**7** Whisk in half the sugar, fold in the remainder with the tablespoon.

**8** Spoon the meringue on top of the ice cream and stand the oranges on an oven-proof dish or plate or tin.

**9** Bake for about 3 minutes only in the centre of a very hot oven.

**10** Serve as quickly as possible on the dish or plate on which the meringue was baked or lift from the tin on to a serving plate.

# Lemon and banana flan

This flan uses biscuit crumbs and a very delicious lemon and banana mixture. It would be splendid for a special party. It does not need cooking, but you must start making it in good time so that the jelly will set.

**You will need:**

| | |
|---|---|
| *lemon jelly* | 1 packet |
| *water* | 284 ml (½ pint) |
| *double cream* | 142 ml (¼ pint) |
| *lemon* | 1 |
| *bananas* | 3 |
| *sugar* | 1 tablespoon |

for the flan case:

| | |
|---|---|
| *digestive biscuits* | 150 grammes (6 oz) |
| *butter or margarine* | 75 grammes (3 oz) |
| *caster sugar* | 50 grammes (2 oz) |

*These ingredients will make 6 servings.*

**You will use:**
plates for ingredients, 3 basins (1 must be heat resistant), kettle, heat resistant measuring jug, wooden spoon, egg whisk, sharp knife, chopping board, lemon squeezer, fork, tablespoon, greaseproof paper, rolling pin, serving plate, flan ring (not essential), teaspoon.

**For success:**
Make quite sure the jelly is beginning to set before you add the cream and mashed bananas.

**1** Separate the pieces of the jelly tablet and put into the heat resistant basin.

**2** Put the water in the kettle and either light the gas burner or switch on the electric hotplate or electric kettle.

**3** Let the water come to boiling point, then pour it (or ask a grown-up to do this) into the measuring jug to give the right amount.

**4** Pour the water over the jelly and stir with a wooden spoon until dissolved.

**5** Allow the jelly to cool, then put it in the refrigerator and leave until it *begins to stiffen slightly*. This will take at least 1½–2 hours; do not let it become too stiff; for if the jelly sets too early it is not possible to blend in the whipped cream, lemon juice and bananas as stages 6 to 9.

**6** Pour the cream into a basin and whisk it until it just stands up in peaks; do not over-beat cream for this spoils it.

**7** Cut the lemon in half and squeeze out the juice.

**8** Put the bananas into the third basin and mash them with a fork, then add the sugar and the lemon juice; mix well together.

**9** Fold the mashed bananas and then *half* the whipped cream into the partly set jelly. Put the basin containing the rest of the cream in a cool place. You need this for the decoration.

**10** Put the jelly mixture back in the refrigerator for a short time to become stiffer.

**11** Meanwhile prepare the flan case.

**12** Put the digestive biscuits on to a sheet of greaseproof paper or better still into a plastic or greaseproof bag (using a bag makes less mess than using the sheets of greaseproof paper).

**13** Cover with a second sheet of paper and roll gently but firmly with the rolling pin until you make fine crumbs; leave on the paper for the time being.

**14** Put the butter or margarine and sugar into a basin and cream with a wooden spoon until soft.

**15** Gradually add the biscuit crumbs and stir well (you may find a metal tablespoon easier and better than the wooden spoon).

**16** Form the biscuit mixture into a flan shape, as in the picture. This means making a flat round for the base, then a rim of about 2.5 cm (1 inch) all round. If you have a plain 20 cm (8 inch) flan ring you can put this on the serving plate and make the flan shape in it, then lift it away very carefully.

**17** Put the flan in a cool place to set – this will take about ½ hour. At the same time make sure the jelly mixture is not becoming too firm.

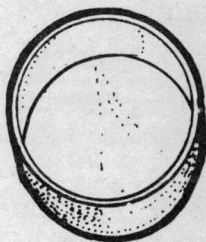

**18** Spoon the jelly mixture into the flan case.

**19** Top with the rest of the whipped cream.

## To make a change

Instead of the lemon and banana mixture, you can use an orange filling – on page 171 – or an orange and apple filling.

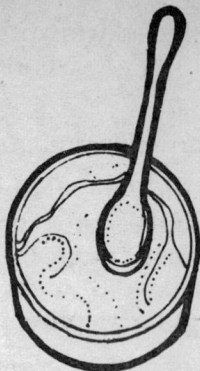

## Did you know?

Whipped evaporated milk can be used instead of cream. This is the easiest way to whip the milk.

Chill the unopened can of milk in the refrigerator for at least 1 hour, open this with a can opener (or ask an adult to do this).

Pour the evaporated milk into a large mixing bowl and beat hard with an egg whisk until light and fluffy.

# Orange flan

Use an orange jelly instead of the lemon jelly in the recipe on pages 167 to 170; you do not need the lemon. Use a small can of mandarin oranges instead of the bananas.

1  Dissolve the orange jelly in 284 ml (½ pint) boiling water as described in stages 1–4 on page 168.

2  Open the can of mandarin oranges, strain through a sieve. Add 142 ml (¼ pint) liquid from the can to the dissolved jelly, together with the mandarin orange segments.

3  Allow the jelly mixture to stiffen slightly, then fold *half* the whipped cream into this, as in stage 9, and continue to the end of the recipe.

## *Orange and apple flan*

1  Dissolve the orange jelly as stage 1 above.

2  Add 225 ml (7½ fl oz) sweetened apple purée. Continue as stage 3.

# Did you know?

*Creaming* margarine and sugar in recipes is quite hard work; you will make it easier if:

**1** You choose the modern soft (luxury) margarines or vegetable fats. These are so soft that you do not need to work hard at all. In fact you can put all the ingredients of the cake recipe (for example orange upside down cake) into a mixing bowl and cream them together for about 2 minutes; this saves a great deal of time. If using an electric mixer allow about 1 minute on low speed.

**2** When *creaming* margarine or other fat, always stand the mixing bowl on a teacloth, this will save it slipping as you beat the mixture with a wooden spoon.

**3** When *whisking* egg whites, or *rubbing* fat into flour or *kneading* a mixture you can stand the mixing bowl on a teacloth just as described under point 2.

**4** When *whisking* egg whites you should remove the eggs from the refrigerator or cold larder and keep them at room temperature for 1 hour before separating the egg yolks. If egg whites are too cold they will not whisk well. Use a high speed for whisking egg whites in an electric mixer, see also page 14.

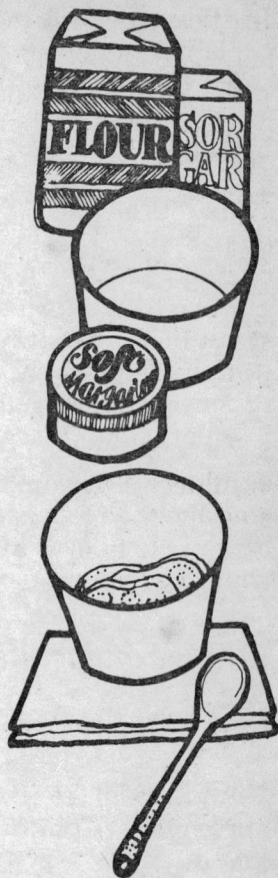

# Did you know?

The best way to line cake tins with paper is as follows:

**1** Cut a round or square the size of the base of the tin – to do this put the tin over the paper and draw round it.

**2** Put this on one side while you prepare the paper for the sides of the tin. Fold the paper to give a doube band round the inside of the tin. Make slits about 1 cm (½ inch) deep at 1 cm (½ inch) intervals along one side of the paper.

**3** Put this into the cake tin and fold the bottom part so the slits 'spread out' and give a neat fit at the bottom edge of the tin.

**4** Put the round or square on top of this.

# Did you know?

There are two ways of greasing cake tins or the paper-lined cake tins:

**1** Melt a little fat in a saucepan or old basin standing in hot water. Dip a pastry brush in the melted fat and brush round the bottom and sides of the tin. Instead of melted fat you could use oil.

**1** Do not melt the fat.
Take a small piece of greaseproof paper. Put a very little fat on this and rub it round the bottom and sides of the tin.

# INDEX